24-Hour Crochet Projects

by Rita Weiss

Sterling Publishing Co., Inc.
New York

LIBRARY OF CONGRESS CATALOGING-IN-PUBLICATION DATA

Published by Sterling Publishing Co., Inc.
387 Park Avenue South, New York, NY 10016
© 2005 by The Creative Partners, LLC™
Distributed in Canada by Sterling Publishing
c/o Canadian Manda Group, 165 Dufferin Street
Toronto, Ontario, Canada M6K 3H6
Distributed in Great Britain by Chrysalis Books Group PLC
The Chrysalis Building, Bramley Road, London W10 6SP, England
Distributed in Australia by Capricorn Link (Australia) Pty. Ltd.
P.O. Box 704, Windsor, NSW 2756, Australia

ISBN 1-4027-1377-0

Introduction

Crocheting is easy, fast, and fun!

Just think what you can make in only 24 hours or less of crocheting— a cute little sweater top, a trendy scarf, a hat, a must-have purse—and every one of the projects in this great book.

Crocheting is easy to take up and to put down; it will go with you quite happily to a doctor's appointments, a boring meeting, a child's soccer game. Our patterns are easy, so they don't require your full concentration.

As a crocheter, you will be amazed at how quickly you can create fabulous projects that will have your friends and family begging for their own, just like yours.

Just in case you can't remember how to crochet, or if you are confused about what those abbreviations and symbols mean, spend a little time with our "Refresher Course" starting on page 116. Then you'll be ready to go.

To speed you along, we tell you how much time will be required to finish a project. Don't be dismayed, however, if it takes you longer. It's not a race, and crocheting is time well spent. Whether you crochet for just one hour a day, or for hours at a time, 24 of those precious hours will reward you with a wide variety of creations you'll love.

CONTENTS

GLITTERING GOLD

ALL STRIPES

HAT SHOPPE

HIPSTER SCARF

SUNNY DAYS TANK TOP

LITTLE DOILIES

MUST HAVE BLOUSE

SUNSHINE BLOCKS

ABSOLUTELY PRECIOUS

BABY DREAMS

HELMET HAT WARDROBE

KEYHOLE SCARF

Gallery of Projects

GLITTERING GOLD

Designed by Sandy Scoville

Wear this outfit, and you'll be the glittering star of the ball. The glitter comes from the use of a yarn that has a gold metallic thread running through it, just the perfect thing to catch the light as all eyes turn toward the glamorous wearer. So only wear this outfit if you love to bask in the limelight.

PATTERN APPEARS ON PAGE 58

ALL STRIPES

What could be more fun than wearing this cheery scarf—especially when the weather turns cold? Why, it's probably much more fun to crochet it. The entire scarf is worked with single crochet stitches and seven different colors. A great way to use up all of the bits and pieces left over from other projects—or a great excuse to buy seven brand new yarns.

PATTERN APPEARS ON PAGE 62

HAT SHOPPE

Designed by Denise Black

Shop for the latest in headgear right here instead of in a high-end store. From the "Biker's Beret" to the "High Roller," here are the perfect additions to anyone's fashionable wardrobe. Remember the hat makes the woman.

PATTERNS APPEAR ON PAGE 63

15

HIPSTER SCARF

Designed by Sandy Scoville

A break from tradition: who says that a scarf has to be worn around your neck? Why not around your hips where it adds a real fashion statement. The wonderful new tape yarn creates a look that is truly "now".

PATTERN APPEARS ON PAGE 71

SUNNY DAYS TANK TOP

Designed by Denise Black

Enjoy the warmth of the sun when you wear this delightful tank top with skirts, pants or jeans. Here is a top that is quick and easy to finish and one that is sure to elicit compliments all summer long.

PATTERN APPEARS ON PAGE 72

LITTLE DOILIES

Designed by Sandy Scoville

A little thread, a crochet hook, a few hours of work, and you can create a masterpiece that will become a treasured family heirloom. Make just one, or crochet all six. Like eating potato chips—once you start, you'll want to finish the whole bag.

PATTERN APPEARS ON PAGE 74

MUST HAVE BLOUSE

Designed by Denise Black

Sweet as a summer sky, this beautiful blouse is easy and fun to make. It's just as easy to wear because it has that magical ability to blend well with every outfit. The perfect addition to a summer wardrobe.

PATTERN APPEARS ON PAGE 81

SUNSHINE BLOCKS

Designed by Denise Black

*A lush, velvety yarn makes this afghan a delight to curl up
under. Its light weight will make it the perfect afghan to
take to the beach house for those cloudy summer days
when the only sunshine will be that which comes from
the bright warm color of the afghan.*

PATTERN APPEARS ON PAGE 84

ABSOLUTELY PRECIOUS

Designed by Denise Black

What baby wouldn't be delighted to wear this outfit? And what mother wouldn't be delighted to receive this as a gift of your labor. The pretty button bows provide the perfect touch to a perfect outfit.

PATTERN APPEARS ON PAGE 86

BABY DREAMS

Designed by Denise Black

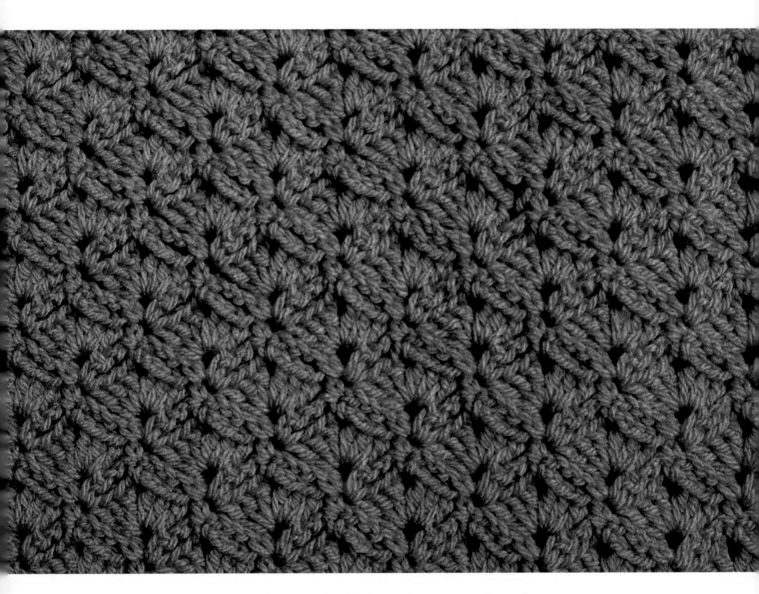

*Wrap up that cherished baby in this warm and comfy
baby afghan. The stitch is a fun one to do, and because
you can make it so quickly it's the perfect last-minute gift
to complete the new baby's wardrobe.*

PATTERN APPEARS ON PAGE 88

HELMET HAT WARDROBE

Designed by Sandy Scoville

There'll be no frostbitten ears in your family, if you brighten up a cold winter's day with one of these colorful helmets featuring bright yarns and textured stitches. Mom, dad and the kids will make good use of these hats when the frosty breezes begin to blow.

PATTERN APPEARS ON PAGE 89

31

KEYHOLE SCARF

Designed by Carol Mansfield

With a special keyhole design that keeps the scarf in place, wintry winds won't blow off this pretty scarf. Long and lovely, you can wear it with a coat, jacket or a warm sweater on cold days and still be stylish.

PATTERN APPEARS ON PAGE 96

AROUND THE BLOCK AFGHAN

Designed by Sandy Scoville

*Make this afghan as big or small as you please. Start in the center
and keep crocheting around and around until you run out of time
or yarn. Use the colors shown here or choose colors that coordinate
with your home décor, or use only two colors, one for the squares
and one for the contrasting trim for each square.*

PATTERN APPEARS ON PAGE 97

INSTANT GRATIFICATION PURSE

Designed by Kathleen Power Johnson

PATTERN APPEARS ON PAGE 98

Make it in a instant;
wear it all day. This trendy
purse will accompany you
from holiday festivities to
summer fun. You'll love
the cord yarn which adds
luster and texture to
this project.

TRENDY TOP

Designed by Denise Black

Be a starlet basking in the sun wearing this trendy top. All eyes are on you. The perfect addition to the wardrobe of the young and sun-loving young Miss.

PATTERN APPEARS ON PAGE 99

BLACK TIE PURSE

Designed by Sandy Scoville

He's not the only one who can wear a black tie. This pearl grey chenille bag is accented with a perky black bow. Now you too can wear it to the next black tie affair. If black tie is too formal for you, try this purse in other colors.

PATTERN APPEARS ON PAGE 102

HUGGABLE AFGHAN

This gorgeous deep blue chenille throw projects the deep richness of velvet.
Everyone who has seen this afghan wants to claim ownership because its
rich color and wonderful texture invite you to snuggle under it.

PATTERN APPEARS ON PAGE 103

CRAYON BLOCKS

Designed by Sandy Scoville

*Color, color everywhere, right out of the crayon box. This
sweater is sure to delight any child with its bold swatches
of colors combined with a carefree ease of wearing.*

PATTERN APPEARS ON PAGE 104

THE LITTLE BLACK BAG

Designed by Sandy Scoville

True elegance! Northing could be more rich to accent your evening costume. The lovely texture and color of the yarn are accented with a dramatic button and tassel.

PATTERN APPEARS ON PAGE 107

LITTLE FAN'S ONESIE

Designed by Denise Black

The little sports fan will be ready for the big game when dressed up in this cute outfit. Pick your favorite team's colors and your favorite player's number to make this a fun statement. Play ball!

PATTERN APPEARS ON PAGE 108

EVERYTHING'S ROSIE

Designed by Denise Black

Wear this dramatic halter alone or pair it with the lacy cardigan. They are both crocheted in a soft velvety yarn that will drape beautifully.

PATTERN APPEARS ON PAGE 110

RED HOT PURSE

Designed by Sandy Scoville

Really, really red, the power color of this chenille bag tells the world that you are someone to be reckoned with. It is the perfect size for carrying all of your essentials for a specially elegant evening.

PATTERN APPEARS ON PAGE 114

THINK MINK

Designed by Denise Black

If you don't want to wear the real thing, this faux-mink
headband will be a wonderful accessory. Quick and easy
to make, it's fun to create from wonderful chenille yarn.
Add a touch of elegance to any outfit.

PATTERN APPEARS ON PAGE 115

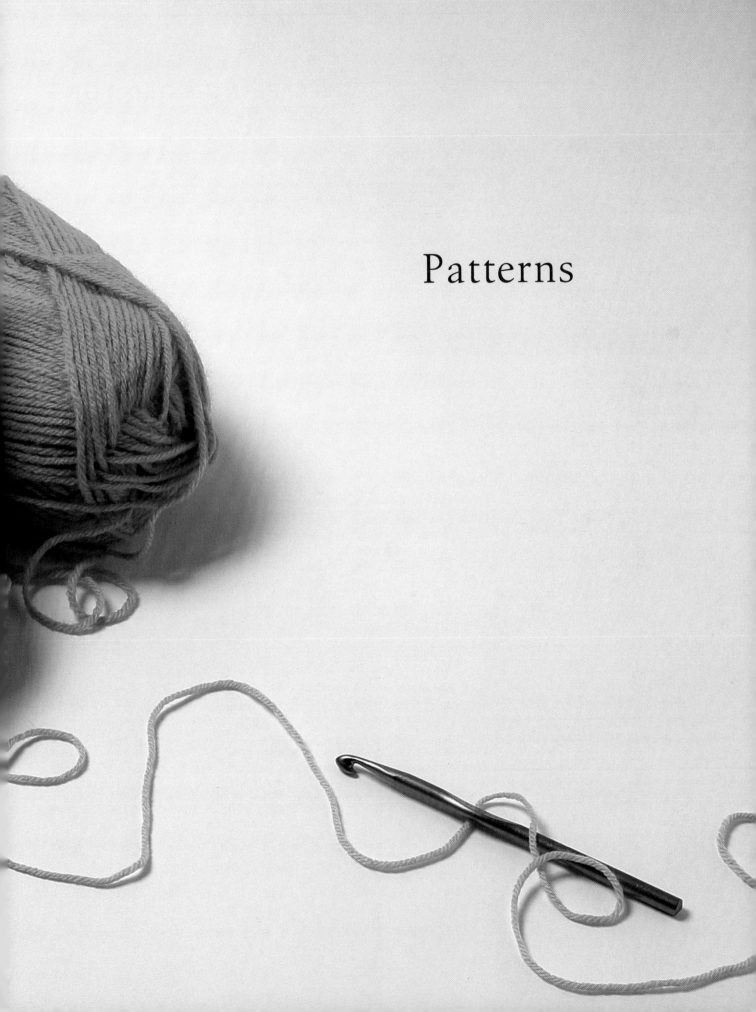

Patterns

GLITTERING GOLD TOP

Designed by Sandy Scoville

Note: *Instructions are written for size Small; changes for sizes Medium and Large are in parentheses.*

Size:	Small	Medium	Large
Body Chest Measurements:	32"–34"	34"–36"	33"–38"
Finished Chest Measurement:	34"	36"	38"

Time to make: About 12 hours

MATERIALS:

Worsted weight yarn, 8 (8¾, 9½) oz. gold with metallic gold thread

Note: *Photographed model made with Lion Brand Glitterspun,® #170 Gold*

Size G (4 mm) crochet hook, or size required for gauge

Size F (3.75 mm) crochet hook

Size 16 tapestry needle

GAUGE:

4 dc = 1"

5 dc rows = 2"

Instructions:

BACK:

Lower Trim:

With larger size hook, ch 70 (74, 78).

Row 1 (right side): Sc in 2nd ch from hook and in each rem ch: 69 (73, 77) sc. Ch 1, turn.

Row 2: Sc in first 2 sc; * ch 5, sk next sc, sc in next 3 sc; rep from * 15 (16, 17) times; ch 5, sk next sc, sc in next 2 sc: 17 (18, 19) ch-5 sps. Ch 1, turn.

Row 3: Sc in first sc; * ch 3, sk next sc, sc in next ch-5 sp, ch 3, sk next sc, sc in next sc; rep from * across: 34 (36, 38) ch-3 sps. Ch 1, turn.

Row 4: Sc in first sc and in next ch-3 sp;

* ch 5, sk next sc, sc in next ch-3 sp, in next sc, and in next ch-3 sp; rep from * 15 (16, 17) times; ch 5, sk next sc, sc in next ch-3 sp and in next sc: 17 (18, 19) ch-5 sps. Ch 1, turn.

Row 5: Sc in first sc; * ch 7, sk next sc, next ch-5 sp, and next sc; in next sc work (sc, ch 5, sc); rep from * 15 (16, 17) times; ch 7, sk next sc, next ch-5 sp, and next sc, sc in next sc. Finish off.

Body:

Hold trim with right side facing and beg ch at top; with larger size hook, join in first unused lp of beg ch of lower trim.

Row 1 (right side): Ch 3 (counts as a dc), dc in each rem unused lp: 69 (73, 77) dc. Ch 3 (counts as first dc on following rows), turn.

Row 2: Dc in each dc and in 3rd ch of beg ch-3. Ch 3, turn.

Row 3: Dc in each dc and in 3rd ch of turning ch-3. Ch 3, turn.

Rows 4 through 18 (20, 20): Rep Row 3. At end of last row, do not ch 3. Ch 1, turn.

Row 19 (21, 21): Sl st in each dc and in 3rd ch of turning ch-3. Ch 1, turn.

BACK BODICE SHAPING:

Row 1 (wrong side): Working in dc on Row 18 (20, 20) behind sl sts on prev row, sc in each dc and in 3rd ch of turning ch-3: 69

(73, 77) sc. Ch 1, turn.

Row 2 (right side): Sc in each sc. Ch 1, turn.

Rows 3 through 11 (13, 13): Sc in each sc. At end of last row, do not ch 1. Turn.

ARMHOLE SHAPING:

Row 1 (right side): Sl st in first 4 sc; dec over next 2 sc (to work dec: draw up lp in each of next 2 sc, YO and draw through all 3 lps on hook: dec made); sc in next 57 (61, 65) sc; dec over next 2 sc: 59 (63, 67) sc. Ch 1, turn, leaving rem 4 sc unworked.

Row 2: Sk first sc, sc in each sc to last 2 sc; dec: 57 (61, 65). Ch 1, turn.

Row 3: Rep Rnd 2. At end of row: 55 (59, 63) sc. Ch 1, turn.

Row 4: Sc in each sc. Ch 1, turn.

Rows 5 through 6 (8, 8): Rep Rnds 3 and 4. At end of last row: 53 (55, 59) sc. Ch 1, turn.

RIGHT BACK SHOULDER SHAPING:

Row 1 (right side): Sk first sc, sc in next 8 (8, 10) sc, dec over next 2 sc: 9 (9, 11) sc. Ch 1, turn, leaving rem sc unworked.

Row 2: Sk first sc, sc in next 6 (6, 8) sc, dec over next 2 sc: 7 (7, 9) sc. Ch 1, turn.

Row 3: Sc in each sc. Ch 1, turn.

Rep Row 3 until shoulder measures 7" (7",

8" from underarm shaping, ending by working a wrong-side row. At end of last row, do not ch-1. Finish off.

LEFT BACK SHOULDER SHAPING:

Hold piece with right side facing; sk next 31 (33, 33) sts from right back shoulder; with larger size hook, join in next sc.

Row 1 (right side): Sk joining sc, sc in next 8 (8, 10) sc, dec over next 2 sc: 9 (9, 11) sc.

Ch 1, turn.

Row 2: Sk first sc, sc in next 6 (6, 8) sc, dec over next 2 sc: 7 (7, 9) sc. Ch 1, turn.

Row 3: Sc in each sc. Ch 1, turn.

Rep Row 3 until shoulder measures 7" (7", 8") from underarm shaping, ending by working a wrong-side row. At end of last row, do not ch-1.

Finish off and weave in all ends.

FRONT:

Work same as for back to bodice shaping.

RIGHT FRONT BODICE SHAPING:

Row 1 (wrong side): Working in dc on Row 18 (20, 20) behind sl sts on prev row, sc in first 34 (36, 38) dc. Ch 1, turn, leaving rem sts unworked.

Row 2 (right side): Sk first sc, sc in next 6 sc; * 2 sc in next sc, sc in next sc; rep from * 6 times more; sc in each rem sc: 40 (42, 44) sc. Ch 1, turn.

Row 3: Sc in each sc to last 2 sc; dec over last 2 sc: 39 (41, 43) sc. Ch 1, turn.

Row 4: Sk first sc, sc in each rem sc: 38 (40, 42) sc. Ch 1, turn.

Rows 5 through 10 (12, 12): Rep Rows 3 and 4. At end of last row: 32 (32, 34) sc. Ch 1, turn.

Row 11 (13, 13): Rep Row 3. At end of row: 31 (31, 33) sc. Ch 1, turn.

ARMHOLE SHAPING:

Row 1 (right side): Sk first sc, sc in next 24 (24, 26) sc, dec over next 2 sc: 25 (25, 27) sc. Ch 1, turn, leaving rem 4 sts unworked.

Row 2: Sk first sc, sc in each sc to last 2 sc; dec: 23 (23, 25) sc. Ch 1, turn.

Rows 3 through 6: Rep Rnd 2. At end of Row 6: 15 (15, 17) sc. Ch 1, turn.

Row 7: Sk first sc, * dec; sc in next sc; rep from * 3 times more; dec; sc in next 0 (0, 2) sc: 9 (9, 11) sc. Ch 1, turn.

Row 8: Rep Row 2. At end of row: 7 (7, 9) sc. Ch 1, turn.

Row 9: Sc in each sc. Ch 1, turn.

Rep Row 9 until Right Front Bodice measures same as Back. At end of last row, do not ch 1.

Finish off and weave in ends.

LEFT FRONT BODICE SHAPING:

Hold piece with wrong side facing; join yarn in 2nd dc on Row 18 (20, 20) behind sl st.

Row 1 (wrong side): Working in dc on Rnd 18 (20, 20) behind sl sts on prev row, ch 1, sc in same sc as joining, in each rem dc, and in 3rd ch of turning ch-3: 34 (36, 38) sc. Ch 1, turn.

continued on page 60

* dec; sc in next sc; rep from * 3 times more; dec: 9 (9, 11) sc. Ch 1, turn.

Row 8: Rep Row 2; at end of row: 7 (7, 9) sc.

Row 9: Sc in each sc. Ch 1, turn.

Rep Row 9 until left front bodice measures same as back. At end of last row, do not ch 1.

Finish off. Weave in ends.

Sew shoulder and side seams, leaving lower trim open.

ARMHOLE EDGINGS:
Hold top with right side facing you and one underarm at top; with smaller size hook, join in first unused sc to left of side seam.

Rnd 1: Ch 1, sc in same sc as joining, in next sc, in side of each row along armhole edge, and in next 2 unused underarm sc; join in first sc.

Rnd 2: Ch 1, sc in same sc as joining and in next sc; * ch 5, sk next sc, sc in next 3 sc; ch 5, sk next sc; rep from * around; ch 5, sk next sc, sc in each sc to first sc; join.

Rep for other armhole edging.

NECKLINE EDGING:
Hold top with right side of back facing you; with smaller size hook, join in side of first row to left of right shoulder seam.

Rnd 1: Ch 1, sc in same sp, in side of each row, and in each unused sc across back, in side of each row to next shoulder seam, in side of each row along left front bodice, in unused dc behind sl st at center, and in side of each row along right front bodice; join in first sc.

Rnd 2: Ch 1, sc in same sc as joining and in next sc; ch 5, sk next sc; * sc in next 3 sc, ch 5, sk next sc; rep from * around neckline; sc in each sc to first sc; join in first sc.

Finish off. Weave in ends.

Row 2 (right side): Sc in first 12 (14, 16) sc; * 2 sc in next sc, sc in next sc; rep from * 6 times more; sc in next 6; dec: 40 (42, 44) sc. Ch 1, turn.

Row 3: Sk first sc, sc in each rem sc: 39 (41, 43) sc. Ch 1, turn.

Row 4: Sc in each sc to last 2 sc; dec: 38 (40, 42) sc. Ch 1, turn.

Rows 5 through 10 (12, 12): Rep Rows 3 and 4. At end of last row: 32 (32, 34) sc. Ch 1, turn.

Row 11 (13, 13): Rep Row 3. At end of row: 31 (31, 33) sc. Ch 1, turn.

ARMHOLE SHAPING:
Row 1 (right side): Sk first sc, sc in next 24 (24, 26) sc, dec over next 2 sc: 25 (25, 27) sc. Ch 1, turn, leaving rem 4 sts unworked.

Row 2: Sk first sc, sc in each sc to last 2 sc; dec: 23 (23, 25) sc. Ch 1, turn.

Rows 3 through 6: Rep Rnd 2. At end of Row 6: 15 (15, 17) sc. Ch 1, turn.

Row 7: Sk first sc, sc in next 0 (0, 2) sc;

GLITTERING GOLD SHAWL

Designed by Sandy Scoville

Time to make: About 17 hours

SIZE:
About 18 wide x 72" long

MATERIALS:
Worsted weight yarn, 16 oz; gold with metallic gold thread

Note: *Photographed model made with Lion Brand Glitterspun®, #170 Gold*

Size G (4 mm) crochet hook, or size required for gauge

Size 16 tapestry needle

GAUGE:
4 dc = 1"

Instructions:

LOWER TRIM:
Ch 74.

Row 1 (right side): Sc in 2nd ch from hook and in each rem ch: 73 sc. Ch 1, turn.

Row 2: Sc in first 2 sc; * ch 5, sk next sc, sc in next 3 sc; rep from * 16 times; ch 5, sk next sc, sc in next 2 sc: 18 ch-5 sps. Ch 1, turn.

Row 3: Sc in first sc, * ch 3, sk next sc, sc in next ch-5 sp, ch 3, sk next sc, sc in next sc; rep from * across: 36 ch-3 sps. Ch 1, turn.

Row 4: Sc in first sc and in next ch-3 sp; * ch 5, sk next sc, sc in next ch-3 sp, in next sc, and in next ch-3 sp; rep from * 16 times; ch 5, sk next sc, sc in next ch-3 sp and in next sc: 18 ch-5 sps. Ch 1, turn.

Row 5: Sc in first sc; * ch 7, sk next sc, next ch-5 sp, and next sc, in next sc work (sc, ch 5, sc); rep from * 16 times; ch 7, sk next sc, next ch-5 sp, and next sc, sc in next sc. Finish off.

BODY:
Hold trim with right side facing and beg ch at top, join in first unused lp of beg ch.

Row 1 (right side): Sc in same lp and in each rem unused lp: 73 sc. Ch 1, turn.

Row 2: Sc in first sc; * ch 5, sk next 2 sc, sc in next sc; rep from * across: 24 ch-5 sps. Ch 5 (counts as first dc and a ch-2 sp on following rows), turn.

Row 3: Sc in next ch-5 sp; * ch 5, sc in next ch-5 sp; rep from * across; ch 2, dc in next sc: 23 ch-5 sps. Ch 1, turn.

Row 4: Sc in first dc, ch 5, sk next ch-2 sp, sc in next ch-5 sp; * ch 5, sc in next ch-5 sp; rep from * across; ch 5, sc in 3rd ch of turning ch-5. Ch 5, turn.

Rep Rows 3 and 4 until shawl measures about 70", ending by working a Row 3.

ENDING TRIM:

Row 1 (wrong side): Sc in first dc, sc in next ch-2 sp; sc in next sc; * 2 sc in next ch-5 sp; sc in next sc; rep from * to last ch-2 sp; sc in next ch-2 sp; sc in 3rd ch of turning ch-5: 73 sc. Ch 1, turn.

Row 2 (right side): Sc in each sc. Ch 1, turn.

Rows 3 through 6: Rep Rows 2 through 5 of lower trim.

Finish off. Weave in ends.

ALL STRIPES

Time to make: About 9 hours

SIZE:

7" x 72"

MATERIALS:

Light worsted weight yarn, 1 oz red; 2 oz white; 2 oz wheat; 3/4 oz blue; 3/4 oz light green; 1 1/2 oz dark red; 2 oz rose

Note: *Photographed model made with TLC® Amoré™, #3907 Red Velvet, #3103, Vanilla, #3220 Wheat, #3823 Lake Blue, #3625 Celery, #3782 Garnet and #3710 Rose*

Size I (5.5 mm) crochet hook, or size required for gauge

GAUGE:

4 sc = 1"

Instructions:

With red, ch 31.

Row 1: Sc in 3rd ch from hook; * ch 1, skip next ch, sc in next ch. Repeat from * across. Ch 2, turn: 14 ch-1 sps.

Row 2: Skip first sc, * sc in next ch-1 sp, ch 1, skip next sc; rep from * to last sp; sc in ch-2 space. Ch 2 turn.

Rep Row 2 for pattern, following colors sequence below. Work over yarn ends as you work.

* Work the following stripes:

Red: 4 rows

White: 2 rows

Wheat: 4 rows

Blue: 4 rows

Light green: 2 rows

Blue: 2 rows

White: 2 rows

Dark red: 4 rows

White: 2 rows

Rose: 6 rows

White: 2 rows

Wheat: 2 rows

White: 2 rows

Light green: 4 rows

Dark Red: 4 rows

White: 2 rows

Rose: 6 rows

Wheat: 6 rows

Dark red: 2 rows

White: 2 rows

Rep from * three times more.

Work 4 rows of red. Finish off. Weave in ends.

LOVELY LID
PAGE 66

HEADS UP
PAGE 67

HAT SHOPPE

BILLED BEAUTY
PAGE 64

BIKER'S "BERET"
PAGE 69

HIGH ROLLER
PAGE 68

ON THE CUFF
PAGE 70

BILLED BEAUTY

Designed by Denise Black

Time to make: About 4 hours

SIZE:
Fits 20" to 23" head

MATERIALS:
Worsted weight yarn, 3 oz burgundy
Note: *Photographed model made with TLC® Amoré™ #3782 Garnet*
Size H (5 mm) crochet hook, or size required for gauge
Size 16 tapestry needle
7" x 4"- piece of plastic for bill
Matching sewing thread, sewing needle

GAUGE:
First 3 rnds = 4"

PATTERN STITCHES:
Front Post Double Crochet (FPdc): YO, insert hook from front to back to front around post of st indicated, draw up lp, (YO, draw through 2 lps on hook) twice: FPdc made.

Back Post Double Crochet (BPdc): YO, insert hook from back to front to back around post of st indicated, draw up lp, (YO, draw through 2 lps on hook) twice: BPdc made.

Instructions:
Ch 4, join to form a ring.

Rnd 1 (right side)**:** Ch 3 (counts as a dc on this and following rnds), 15 dc in ring; join in 3rd ch of beg ch-3: 16 dc.

Rnd 2: Ch 3, dc in same ch as joining; 2 dc in each dc; join: 32 dc.

Rnd 3: Ch 3, dc in same ch as joining; dc in next dc; * 2 dc in next dc, dc in next dc; rep from * around; join: 48 dc.

Rnd 4: Ch 3, dc in same ch as joining; dc in next 2 dc; * 2 dc in next dc, dc in next 2 dc; rep from * around; join: 64 dc.

Rnd 5: Ch 3, dc in each dc; join.

Rnd 6: Ch 3, dc in same ch as joining; dc in next 3 dc; * 2 dc in next dc, dc in next 3 dc; rep from * around; join: 80 dc.

Rnd 7: Ch 3, dc in each dc; join.

Rnd 8: Ch 3, dc in same ch as joining; dc in next 4 dc; * 2 dc in next dc, dc in next 4 dc; rep from * around; join: 96 dc.

Rnd 9: Ch 3, dc in same ch as joining; dc in next dc; * 2 dc in next dc; dc in next 3 dc, 2 dc in next dc; dc in next dc; rep from * 14 times more; 2 dc in next dc, dc in next 3 dc; join: 128 dc.

Rnd 10: Ch 3, dc in each dc; join.

Rnd 11: Ch 3, dc in next 2 dc; * (YO, insert hook in next st, YO and draw through 2 lps on hook) twice; YO and draw through all 3 lps on hook: dc dec made; dc in next 6 dc; rep from * to last 3 dc; dc in last 3 dc; join-112 dc.

Rnd 12: Ch 3, dc in next dc; * dc dec, dc in next 5 dc; rep from * to last 3 dc; dc in last 3 dc; join: 96 dc.

Rnd 13: Ch 3, dc in each dc; join.

Rnd 14: Ch 3, dc in next dc; * dc dec; dc in next 4 dc; rep from * to last 2 dc; dc in last 2 dc; join: 80 dc.

Rnd 15: Ch 3, dc in each dc; join.

Rnd 16: Ch 1, sc in same ch as joining; sc in next dc, draw up lp in each of next 2 sts, YO and draw through all 3 lps on hook; sc dec made; * sc in next 2 dc, sc dec over next 2 dc; rep from * around; join in first sc: 60 sc.

Rnd 17: Ch 3, dc in each sc; join.

Rnds 18 and 19: Ch 3, FPdc (see Pattern Stitches); in next dc, * BPdc (see Pattern Stitches) in next dc; FPdc in next dc; rep from * around; join.

BILL

First Half

Row 1 (right side)**:** Ch 1, sc in next 30 sts. DO NOT WORK REM STS. Ch 1, turn.

Row 2: Sc dec; sc in each sc to last 2 sc; sc dec: 28 sc. Ch 1, turn.

Rows 3 through 8: Rep Row 2: 16 sc. Ch 1, turn.

Second Half

Row 9 (folding row)**:** Sc in each sc. Ch 1, turn.

Row 10: 2 sc in first sc, sc in each sc to last sc, 2 sc in last sc: 18 sc. Ch 1, turn.

Rows 11 through 16: Rep Row 10: 30 sc at end of row 16. Finish off.

FINISHING

Fold bill in half, wrong sides together. Working in ends of rows through corresponding sts of both halves, join in Row 1 of first half and Row 16 of second half, ch 1, sc in same row as joining, sc in each row to folding row; working along front of bill in corresponding sts of rows 8 and 9, sc in each st; working along next edge of bill in ends of rows through corresponding sts, sc in each row. Cut a piece of plastic to shape of bill and slip inside opening; using a slip stitch sew opening closed.

LOVELY LID

Designed by Denise Black

Back Post Double Crochet (BPdc): YO, insert hook from back to front to back around post of st indicated, draw up lp, (YO, draw through 2 lps on hook) twice: BPdc made.

Instructions:

Ch 4, join to form a ring.

Rnd 1 (right side)**:** Ch 3 (counts as a dc on this and following rnds), 11 dc in ring; join in 3rd ch of beg ch-3: 12 dc.

Rnd 2: Ch 3, dc in joining; 2 dc in each dc; join: 24 dc.

Rnd 3: Ch 3, dc in joining; dc in next dc; * 2 dc in next dc, dc in next dc; rep from * around; join: 36 dc.

Rnd 4: Ch 3, dc in joining; dc in next 2 dc; * 2 dc in next dc, dc in next 2 dc; rep from * around; join: 48 dc.

Rnd 5: Ch 3, dc in each dc; join.

Rnds 6 through 8: Ch 3, X-st (see Pattern Stitches) over next 2 dc; dc in next dc; * X-st over next 2 dc; rep from * around; join.

Rnd 9: Ch 3, dc in each dc; join.

Rnds 10 through 13: Ch 3, FPdc (see Pattern Stitches) around post of next dc; * BPdc (see Pattern Stitches) around post of next dc; FPdc around post of next dc; rep from * around; join.

Finish off. Weave in ends.

Time to make: About 2 hours

SIZE:

Fits 19" to 22" head

MATERIALS:

Bulky brushed mohair type yarn,
   2 ½ oz blue

Note *Photographed model made with Lion Brand Jiffy®, #109 Royal*

Size K (6.5 mm) crochet hook, or size required for gauge

Size 16 tapestry needle

GAUGE:

First 2 rnds = 3"; 6 dc = 2"

PATTERN STITCHES:

Cross Stitch (X-st): Sk next st, dc in next st, dc in skipped st: X-st made.

Front Post Double Crochet (FPdc): YO, insert hook from front to back to front around post of st indicated, draw up lp, (YO, draw through 2 lps on hook) twice: FPdc made.

dc; rep from * around; join: 48 dc.

Rnd 5: Ch 3, dc in same ch as joining; dc in next 3 dc; * 2 dc in next dc, dc in next 3 dc; rep from * around; join: 60 dc.

Rnd 6: Ch 3, dc in same ch as joining; dc in next 4 dc; * 2 dc in next dc, dc in next 4 dc; rep from * around; join: 72 dc.

Rnd 7: Ch 3, working in BLs only, dc in each dc; join.

Rnd 8: Ch 3, dc in each dc; join.

Rnds 9 through 13: Rep Rnd 8.

Rnd 14: Ch 2 (counts as an hdc on this and following rnds), hdc in same ch as joining; hdc in next 3 dc; * 2 hdc in next dc, hdc in next 3 dc; rep from * around; join in 2nd ch of beg ch-2: 90 hdc.

Rnd 15: Ch 2, hdc in same ch as joining; hdc in next 2 hdc; * 2 hdc in next hdc, hdc in next 2 hdc; rep from * around; join: 120 hdc.

Rnd 16: Ch 2, hdc in each hdc; join.

Rnds 17 through 19: Rep Rnd 16.

Rnd 20: Ch 1, sc in same ch as joining and in each hdc around. Finish off. Weave in ends.

HEADS UP

Designed by Denise Black

Time to make: About 2 hours

SIZE:

Fits 20" to 23" head

MATERIALS:

Worsted weight yarn, 3½ oz tan
Note: *Photographed model made with Red Heart® Super Saver®, #2330 Linen*
Size F (3.75 mm) crochet hook, or size required for gauge
Size 16 tapestry needle

GAUGE:

First 2 rnds = 2"

Instructions:

Ch 4.

Rnd 1 (right side)**:** 11 dc in 4th ch from hook (beg 3 skipped chs count as a dc); join in 3rd ch of beg 3 skipped chs: 12 dc.

Rnd 2: Ch 3 (counts as a dc on this and following rnds), dc in same ch as joining; 2 dc in each dc; join: 24 dc.

Rnd 3: Ch 3, dc in same ch as joining; dc in next dc; * 2 dc in next dc, dc in next dc; rep from * around; join: 36 dc.

Rnd 4: Ch 3, dc in same ch as joining; dc in next 2 dc; * 2 dc in next dc, dc in next 2

HIGH ROLLER

Designed by Denise Black

Time to make: About 1½ hours

SIZE:

Fits 20" to 23" head

MATERIALS:

Worsted weight yarn, 5 oz, lavender

Note: *Photographed model made with Red Heart® Hokey Pokey™, #7106 Lt. Plum*

Size N (9.0 mm) crochet hook, or size required for gauge

Size K (6.5 mm) crochet hook

Size 16 tapestry needle

GAUGE:

With larger size hook:
First 2 rnds = 2¼"

Instructions:

HAT:

Note: *Hat is worked with 2 strands of yarn held together.*

CROWN:

With larger size hook and 2 strands of yarn, ch 4; join to form a ring.

Rnd 1 (right side): Ch 3 (counts as a dc on this and following rnds), 11 dc in ring; join in 3rd ch of beg ch-3: 12 dc.

Rnd 2: Ch 3, dc in same ch as joining; 2 dc in each rem dc; join: 24 dc.

Rnd 3: Ch 3, 2 dc in next dc; * dc in next dc, 2 dc in next dc; rep from * around; join: 36 dc.

Rnd 4: Ch 1, sc in same ch as joining; * ch 3, sk next dc, sc in next dc; rep from * 16 times more; ch 3, join in first sc: 18 ch-3 sps.

Rnd 5: Sl st in next ch-3 sp, ch 1, sc in same sp; * ch 3, sc in next ch-3 sp; rep from * 16 times more; ch 3; join in first sc.

Rnds 6 through 13: Rep Rnd 5.

BRIM:

Change to smaller size hook.

Rnd 1 (right side): Ch 2 (counts as an hdc on this and following rnds); * 2 hdc in next ch-3 sp; hdc in next sc; rep from * 16 times more; 2 hdc in next ch-3 sp; join in 2nd ch of beg ch-2: 54 hdc.

Rnd 2: Ch 2; * 2 hdc in next hdc, hdc in next hdc; rep from * 25 times more; 2 hdc in next hdc; join: 81 hdc.

Rnd 3: Ch 2, hdc in each hdc; join.

Rnds 4 and 5: Rep Rnd 3.

Rnd 6: Ch 1, work reverse sc (see page 120) around; join in first sc.

Finish off. Weave in ends.

BIKER'S "BERET"

Designed by Denise Black

Time to make: About 1 hour

SIZE:
Fits 21 to 23" head

MATERIALS:
Worsted weight yarn, 2 oz red

Note: Photographed model made with Red Heart® Super Saver®, #319 Cherry Red
Size I (5.5 mm) crochet hook, or size required for gauge
Size 16 tapestry needle

GAUGE:
First 2 rnds = 2"

Instructions:

Ch 4.

Rnd 1 (right side): 11 dc in 4th ch from hook (beg 3 skipped chs count as a dc); join in 3rd ch of beg 3 skipped chs: 12 dc.

Rnd 2: Ch 3 (counts as a dc on this and following rnds), dc in same ch as joining; 2 dc in each dc; join: 24 dc.

Rnd 3: Ch 3, dc in same ch as joining; 2 dc in each dc; join: 48 dc.

Rnd 4: Ch 3, dc in each dc; join: 48 dc

Rnd 5: Ch 3, dc in same ch as joining; dc in next 5 dc; * 2 dc in next dc, dc in next 5 dc; rep from * around; join: 56 dc.

Rnds 6 through 11: Ch 3, dc in each dc; join: 56 dc.

Rnd 12: Ch 1, sc in same ch as joining and in each dc; join in first sc. Finish off. Weave in ends.

ON THE CUFF

Designed by Denise Black

Time to make: About 3 hours

SIZE:
Fits 20" to 23" head

MATERIALS:
Worsted weight yarn, 3½ ounces, tan
Note: *Photographed model made with Red Heart® Super Saver®, #4334 Buff Flec*
Size F (3.75 mm) crochet hook, or size required for gauge
Size 16 tapestry needle

GAUGE
First 2 rnds = 2"

Instructions
Ch 4.

Rnd 1 (right side): 11 dc in 4th ch from hook (beg 3 skipped chs count as a dc); join in 3rd ch of beg ch-3: 12 dc.

Rnd 2: Ch 3 (counts as a dc on this and following rnds), dc in joining; 2 dc in each dc; join: 24 dc.

Rnd 3: Ch 3, dc in joining; dc in next dc; * 2 dc in next dc, dc in next dc; rep from * around; join: 36 dc.

Rnd 4: Ch 3, dc in joining; dc in next 2 dc; * 2 dc in next dc, dc in next 2 dc; rep from * around; join: 48 dc.

Rnd 5: Ch 3, dc in joining; dc in next 3 dc; * 2 dc in next dc, dc in next 3 dc; rep from * around; join: 60 dc.

Rnd 6: Ch 3, dc in joining; dc in next 4 dc; * 2 dc in next dc, dc in next 4 dc; rep from * around; join: 72 dc.

Rnds 7 through 15: Ch 3, dc in each dc; join.

Rnd 16: Ch 3, dc in each dc; join. Turn.

CUFF
Rnd 17: Ch 2 (counts as first hdc on this and following rnds,) hdc in each dc; join in 2nd ch of turning ch-2.

Rnds 18 through 22: Ch 2, hdc in each hdc; join.

Rnd 23: Ch 1, sc in same ch as joining; sc in each hdc; join in first sc. Finish off .

Weave in ends.

Turn cuff up.

70

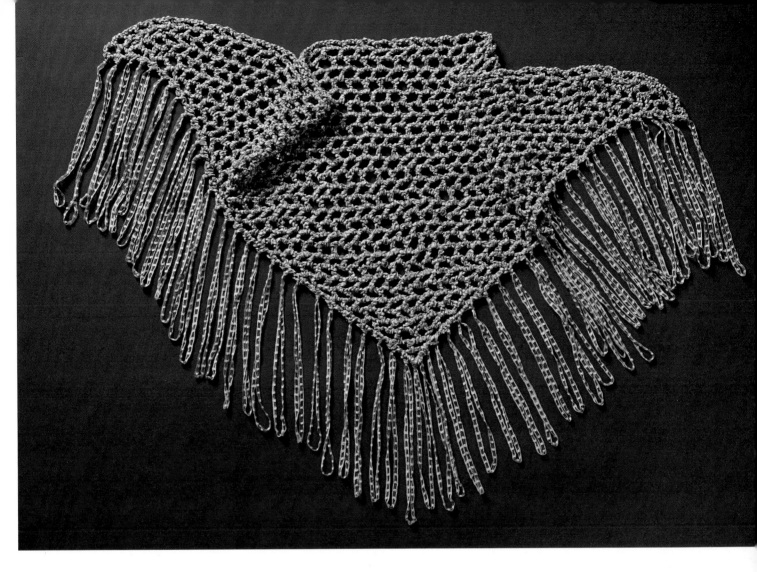

HIPSTER SCARF

Designed by Sandy Scoville

Time to make: 6½ hours

SIZE:
About 46" at top

MATERIALS:
Rayon/polyester, ribbon or "slinky"
  specialty yarn, 275 yds, variegated
Note: *Photographed model made
  with Crystal Palace Choo-Choo,
  #1775 Tangerine*
Size K (6.5 mm) crochet hook or size
  required
  for gauge

GAUGE:
In pattern, two ch-3 sps = 2½"
Note: *Work all stitches loosely.*

Instructions:
Beginning at lower point, ch 7.

Row 1 (right side)**:** Dc in first ch (beginning
skipped 6 chs count as a dc and a ch-3 sp).
Ch 6 (counts as a dc and a ch-3 sp), turn.

Row 2: Dc in ch-3 sp, ch 3, dc in 3rd ch of
beg 6 skipped chs: 2 ch-3 sps. Ch 6, turn.

Row 3: Dc in first dc, ch 3; * dc in next
ch-3 sp, ch 3; rep from * across; dc in 3rd
ch of turning ch-6: 4 ch-3 sps. Ch 6, turn.

Rep Row 3, inc two ch-3 sps each row until
scarf measures about 46" ending by working a right-side row. Ch 1, do not turn.

FRINGE:
Ch 1, working along side edges in sps
made by turning chs and edge dc, sc in
next sp, ch 1, * draw up 10" lp, insert hook
in same sp, draw up a lp, do not draw
through long lp, ch 1; sc in next sp, ch 1,
let long lp slide off opposite end of hook:
fringe made; rep from * to lower point;
work fringe in point and in each sp along
opposite side edge.

Finish off. Weave in ends.

SUNNY DAYS TANK TOP

Designed by Denise Black

Note: *Instructions are written for size Small; changes for larger sizes are in parentheses.*

Size:	Small	Medium	Large
Body Chest Measurements:	30"–32"	34"–36"	38"–40"
Finished Chest Measurement:	35"	39"	43"

Time to make: About 8 hours

MATERIALS:

Sport weight yarn, 12 (14, 16) oz, blue

Note: *Photographed model made with J. & P. Coats® Luster Sheen®, #425 Bluette*

Size F (3.75 mm) crochet hook, or size required for gauge

Size 16 tapestry needle

GAUGE:

(sc, ch 1, dc) twice = 1"

Instructions:

BACK:

Ch 110 (122, 134).

Row 1 (right side): Sc in 2nd ch from hook, sk next 2 chs; * in next ch work (sc, ch 1, dc), sk next 2 chs; rep from * to last ch; sc in last ch: 35 (39, 43) groups of (sc, ch 1, dc). Ch 1, turn.

Row 2: Sc in first sc; * in next ch-1 sp work (sc, ch 1, dc); rep from * to last sc, sc in last sc. Ch 1, turn.

Rep Row 2 until piece measures about 14" (14", 15"), ending by working a wrong side row.

ARMHOLE SHAPING:

Note: *Ch-1 counts as a st.*

Row 1 (right side): Sk first st, sl st in next 8 (11, 11) sts, * in next ch-1 sp work (sc, ch 1, dc); rep from * 28 (30, 34) times more; sl st in next ch-1 sp. Ch 1, turn, leaving rem sts unworked.

For Sizes Small and Medium Only:

Row 2: Sc in first ch-1 sp; * in next ch-1 sp work (sc, ch 1, dc); rep from * to last ch-1 sp; sc in last sp. Ch 1, turn.

Rows 3 and 4: Rep Row 2.

Row 5: Sc in first sc, * in next ch-1 sp work (sc, ch 1, dc); rep from * to last sc; sc in last sc. Ch 1, turn.

Rep Row 5 until armhole measures about 6" ending with a wrong side row.

For Size Large Only:

Row 2: Sc in first ch-1 sp; * in next ch-1 sp work (sc, ch 1, dc); rep from * to last ch-1 sp; sc in last sp. Ch 1, turn.

Rows 3 through 5: Rep Row 2, 3 times more.

Row 6: Sc in first sc, * in next ch-1 sp work (sc, ch 1, dc); rep from * to last sc; sc in last sc. Ch 1, turn.

Rep Row 6 until armhole measures about 6" ending with a wrong side row.

For All Sizes:

RIGHT NECK AND SHOULDER SHAPING:

Row 1 (right side): Sc in first sc; * in next ch-1 sp work (sc, ch 1, dc); rep from * 5 times more; sl st in next ch-1 sp. Ch 2, turn.

Row 2: Sc in next ch-1 sp; * in next ch-1 sp work (sc, ch 1, dc); rep from * 4 times more; sc in next sc. Ch 1, turn.

Row 3: Sc in first sc; * in next ch-1 sp work (sc, ch 1, dc); rep from * 3 times more; sc in next ch-1 sp. Ch 1, turn.

Row 4: Sc in first sc; * in next ch-1 sp work (sc, ch 1, dc); rep from * to last sc; sc in last sc. Ch 1, turn.

Rep Row 4 until armhole measures about 8" (8½", 8½") ending by working a right side row.

Finish off.

LEFT NECK AND SHOULDER SHAPING:

With right side facing sk next 9 (11, 13) ch-1 sps from right neck and shoulder shaping, make slip knot on hook, join with sc in next ch-1 sp.

Row 1 (right side): * In next ch-1 sp work

(sc, ch 1, dc); rep from * to last sc; sc in last sc. Ch 1, turn.

Row 2: Sc in first sc; * in next ch-1 sp work (sc, ch 1, dc); rep from * 4 (4, 4) times more; sc in next ch-1 sp. Ch 2, turn.

Row 3: Sc in next ch-1 sp; * in next ch-1 sp work (sc, ch 1, dc); rep from * 3 times more; sk next sc, sc in next sc. Ch 1, turn.

Row 4: Sc in first sc; * in next ch-1 sp work (sc, ch 1, dc); rep from * to last sc, sc in last sc. Ch 1, turn.

Rep Row 4 until armhole measures about 8" (8½", 8½"). At end of row, do not ch 1. Finish off. Weave in ends.

FRONT

Work same as Back to Armhole Shaping.

ARMHOLE SHAPING:

Note: Ch-1 counts as a st.

Row 1 (right side)**:** Sk first st, sl st in next 8 (11, 11) sts, * in next ch-1 sp work (sc, ch 1, dc); rep from * 28 (30, 34) times more; sl st in next ch-1 sp. Ch 1, turn, leaving rem sts unworked.

For Sizes Small and Medium Only:

Row 2: Sc in first ch-1 sp; * in next ch-1 sp work (sc, ch 1, dc); rep from * to last ch-1 sp; sc in last sp. Ch 1, turn.

Rows 3 and 4: Rep Row 2.

Row 5: Sc in first sc, * in next ch-1 sp work (sc, ch 1, dc); rep from * to last sc; sc in last sc. Ch 1, turn.

Rep Row 5 until armhole measures about 3" ending with a wrong side row.

For Size Large Only:

Row 2: Sc in first ch-1 sp; * in next ch-1 sp work (sc, ch 1, dc); rep from * to last ch-1 sp; sc in last sp. Ch 1, turn.

Rows 3 through 5: Rep Row 2, 3 times more.

Row 6: Sc in first sc, * in next ch-1 sp work (sc, ch 1, dc); rep from * to last sc; sc in last sc.

Rep Row 2 until armhole measures about 3" ending with a wrong side row.

For All Sizes:

LEFT NECK AND SHOULDER SHAPING:

Row 1 (right side)**:** Sc in first sc; * in next ch-1 sp work (sc, ch 1, dc); rep from * 5 times more; sl st in next ch-1 sp. Ch 2, turn.

Row 2: Sc in next ch-1 sp; * in next ch-1 sp work (sc, ch 1, dc); rep from * 4 times more; sc in next sc. Ch 1, turn.

Row 3: Sc in first sc; * in next ch-1 sp work (sc, ch 1, dc); rep from * 3 times more; sc in next sc. Ch 1, turn.

Row 4: Sc in first sc; * in next ch-1 sp work (sc, ch 1, dc); rep from * to last sc; sc in last sc. Ch 1, turn.

Rep Row 4 until piece measures same as back ending with a right side row. Finish off.

RIGHT NECK AND SHOULDER SHAPING:

With right side facing sk next 9 (11, 13) ch-1 sps from right neck and shoulder shaping,

make slip knot on hook, join with sc in next ch-1 sp.

Row 1 (right side)**:** * In next ch-1 sp work (sc, ch 1, dc); rep from * to last sc; sc in last sc. Ch 1, turn.

Row 2: Sc in first sc; * in next ch-1 sp work (sc, ch 1, dc); rep from * 4 times more; sc in next ch-1 sp. Ch 2, turn.

Row 3: Sc in next ch-1 sp; * in next ch-1 sp work (sc, ch 1, dc); rep from * 3 times more; sk next sc, sc in next sc. Ch 1, turn.

Row 4: Sc in first sc; * in next ch-1 sp work (sc, ch 1, dc); rep from * to last sc, sc in last sc. Ch 1, turn.

Rep Row 4 until piece measures same as back, ending with a right side row. At end of last row, do not ch 1. Finish off. Weave in ends.

ASSEMBLY:

Sew shoulder and side seams.

CIRCLES AND STARS PAGE 75

LACEY LOVELY PAGE 76

RING AROUND THE CIRCLE PAGE 77

HIDDEN PINEAPPLES PAGE 78

DIAMONDS IN THE SQUARE PAGE 79

PRETTY PINWHEEL PAGE 80

CIRCLES AND STARS

Designed by Sandy Scoville

Time to make: About 1 hour

SIZE:

6" diameter

MATERIALS:

Bedspread-weight crochet thread,
 100 yds cream

Size 7 (1.5 mm) steel crochet hook, or size
 required for gauge

GAUGE:

8 dc = 1"

Instructions

Ch 4, join to form a ring.

Rnd 1: Ch 1, in ring work (sc, ch 3) 6 times;
join in first sc: 6 ch-3 sps.

Rnd 2: Sl st in first ch of next ch-3 sp, ch 1,
in same sp work (sc, ch 3, sc); * in next
ch-3 sp work (sc, ch 3, sc); rep from
* 4 times more; join.

Rnd 3: Sl st in first ch of next ch-3 sp, ch 1,
in same sp work (sc, ch 3, sc); ch 5; * in
next ch-3 sp work (sc, ch 3, sc); ch 5; rep
from * 4 times more; join.

Rnd 4: Sl st in first ch of next ch-3 sp, ch 1,
in same sp work (sc, ch 3, sc); ch 7, sk next
ch-5 sp; * in next ch-3 sp work (sc, ch 3,
sc); ch 7, sk next ch-5 sp; rep from * 4
times more; join.

Rnd 5: Ch 5, sk next ch-3 sp, sl st in next
sc; in next ch-7 sp work (sc, hdc, 5 dc, hdc,
sc): shell made; * sl st in next sc, ch 5, sk
next ch-3 sp, sl st in next sc, shell in next
ch-7 sp; rep from * 4 times more; join in
joining sl st.

Rnd 6: Sl st in first 2 chs of next ch-5 sp, ch
1, sc in same sp; ch 5, sc in BL of 3rd dc of
next shell, ch 5; * sc in next ch-5 sp, ch 5,
sc in BL of 3rd dc of next shell, ch 5; rep
from * 4 times more; join: 12 ch-5 sps.

Rnd 7: Sl st in next 2 chs of next ch-5 sp,
ch 1, sc in same sp; ch 5, sc in next ch-5 sp,
ch 7; * sc in next ch-5 sp, ch 5, sc in next
ch-5 sp, ch 7; rep from * 4 times more;
join: 6 ch-7 sps .

Rnd 8: Sl st in next ch-5 sp, ch 1, in same
sp work (sc, ch 3, sc, ch 5, sc, ch 3, sc);
shell in next ch-7 sp; * in next ch-5 sp work
(sc, ch 3, sc, ch 5, sc, ch 3, sc); shell in next
ch-7 sp; rep from * 4 times more; join.

Rnd 9: Sl st in next ch-3 sp, ch 1, sc in
same sp; ch 7, sk next ch-5 sp, sc in next
ch-3 sp; * † ch 5, sc in BL of 3rd dc of next
shell, ch 5 †; sc in next ch-3 sp, ch 7, sk
next ch-5 sp, sc in next ch-3 sp; rep from *
4 times more, then rep from † to † once;
join.

Rnd 10: Sl st in next ch-7 sp, ch 1, shell in
same sp; * † in next ch-5 sp work (sc, ch 3,
sc, ch-5, sc); ch 3, in next ch-5 sp work (sc,
ch 5, sc, ch 3, sc) †; shell in next ch-7 sp;
rep from * 4 times more, then rep from †
to † once; join: 6 shells.

Rnd 11: Sl st in next hdc, in next 2 dc, and
in BL of next dc of next shell, ch 1, sc in
same lp; * † ch 7, sk next ch-3 sp, sc in
next ch-5 sp, ch 5, sk next ch-3 sp, sc in
next ch-5 sp, ch 7, sk next ch-3 sp †; sc in
BL of 3rd dc of next shell; rep from * 4
times more, then rep from † to † once; join.

Rnd 12: Sl st in next ch-7 sp, ch 1, shell in
same sp; * † in next ch-5 sp work (sc, ch 3,
sc, ch 5, sc, ch 3, sc) †; shell in each of next
2 ch-7 sps; rep from * 4 times more, then
rep from † to † once; shell in next ch-7 sp;
join. Finish off. Weave in ends.

LACEY LOVELY

Designed by Sandy Scoville

Time to make: About 1 hour

SIZE:

5½" diameter

MATERIALS:

Bedspread-weight crochet thread,
 100 yds cream
Size 7 (1.5 mm) steel crochet hook, or size
 required for gauge

GAUGE:

8 dc = 1"

Instructions:

Ch 6, join to form a ring.

Rnd 1: Ch 1, 12 sc in ring; join in first sc.

Rnd 2: Ch 4 (counts as a dc and a ch-1 sp),
working in BL(s) only, * dc in next sc, ch 1;
rep from * around; join in 3rd ch of beg
ch-4.

Rnd 3: Sl st in next ch-1 sp, ch 2, keeping
last lp of each dc on hook, 2 dc in same sp,
YO and draw through all 3 lps on hook:
beg cluster made; ch 3; * keeping last lp of
each dc on hook, 3 dc in next ch-1 sp, YO
and draw through all 4 lps on hook: cluster
made; ch 3; rep from * around; join in first
cluster: 12 clusters

Rnd 4: Sl st in next ch-3 sp, ch 1, 4 sc in
same sp; 4 sc in each rem ch-3 sp; join:
48 sc.

Rnd 5: Ch 1, sc in same sc; * ch 5, sk next
2 sc, sc in next sc, ch 5, sc in next sc; rep
from * 10 times more; ch 5, sk next 2 sc, sc
in next sc, ch 5, join: 24 ch-5 sps.

Rnd 6: Sl st in first 2 chs of next ch-5 sp
and in same sp, ch 3, keeping last lp of
each tr on hook, 2 tr in same sp, YO and
draw through all 3 lps on hook: beg tr
cluster made; ch 5, sc in next ch-5 sp, ch 5;
* keeping last lp of each tr on hook, 3 tr in
next ch-5 sp, YO and draw through all 4 lps
on hook: tr cluster made; ch 5, sc in next
ch-5 sp, ch 5; rep from * 10 times more;
join in beg tr cluster: 12 tr clusters.

Rnd 7: Ch 1, sc in same cluster; * † ch 3, sc
in next ch-5 sp, ch 5, sc in next ch-5 sp, ch
3 †; sc in next cluster; rep from * 10 times
more, then rep from † to † once; join.

Rnd 8: Sl st in first ch of next ch-3 sp, ch 1,
sc in same sp; ch 5, keeping last lp of each
tr on hook, 4 tr in next ch-5 sp, YO and
draw through all 5 lps on hook: 4-tr cluster
made; ch 3, sl st in top of same 4-tr cluster:
picot made; ch 5, sc in next ch-3 sp, ch 3;
* sc in next ch-3 sp, ch 5, 4-tr cluster in
next ch-5 sp, picot; ch 5, sc in next ch-3 sp,
ch 3; rep from * 10 times more; join. Finish
off and weave in ends.

RING AROUND THE CIRCLE

Designed by Sandy Scoville

Time to make: About 1½ hours

SIZE:
4½" diameter

MATERIALS:
Bedspread weight crochet thread,
  100 yds cream
Size 7 (1.5 mm) steel crochet hook or size
  required for gauge

GAUGE:
8 dc = 1"

PATTERN STITCHES
Lover's Knot (LK): Draw up lp on hook
⅜", YO and draw through ⅜" lp just
made; insert hook in lp on left side (see
page 120), YO and draw through, YO and
draw through 2 lps on hook.

Double Lover's Knot (DLK): * Draw up
lp on hook ⅜", YO and draw through ⅜"
lp just made; insert hook in lp on left side
(see page 120), YO and draw through, YO
and draw through 2 lps on hook; rep from
* once more: DLK made.

Instructions:
Ch 4, join to form a ring.

Rnd 1: Ch 1, 8 sc in ring; join in first sc.

Rnd 2: Ch 1, working in BLs only, 2 sc in
same sc and in each rem sc; join in first sc:
16 sc.

Rnd 3: Ch 1, working in BLs only, sc in
same sc, LK (see Pattern Stitches); sk next
sc; * sc in next sc, LK, sk next sc; rep from
* around; join in first sc: 8 LK.

Rnd 4: Ch 1, working in BLs only, sc in
same sc; ch 5, sk next LK; * sc in next sc, ch
5, sk next LK; rep from * around; join in
first sc: 8 ch-5 sps.

Rnd 5: Sl st in next ch-5 sp, ch 1, 5 sc in
same ch-5 sp and in each rem ch-5 sp; join
in first sc: 40 sc.

Rnd 6: Ch 1, working in BLs only, sc in
same sc, LK; sk next sc; * sc in next sc, LK,
sk next sc; rep from * around; join in first
sc: 20 LKs.

Rnd 7: Ch 1, sc in same sc; ch 3, sk next
LK; * sc in next sc, ch 3, sk next LK; rep
from * around; join in first sc: 20 ch-3 sps.

Rnd 8: Sl st in next ch-3 sp, ch 1, 4 sc in
same sp and in each rem sp; join in first sc:
80 sc.

Rnd 9: Ch 1, working in BLs only, sc in
same sc; in next sc work (hdc, dc); in next
sc work (dc, hdc); sc in next sc; * sc in next
sc, in next sc work (hdc, dc); in next sc work
(dc, hdc); sc in next dc; rep from * around;
join in first sc: 120 sts.

Rnd 10: Ch 1, working in BLs only, sc in
same sc; * DLK (see Pattern stitches); sk
next 4 sts, sc in next 2 sc; rep from * 18
times more; DLK; sk next 4 sts, sc in next sc;
join in first sc: 20 DLKs.

Rnd 11: Ch 8 (counts as a dc and a ch-5
sp); * sk next DLK, keeping last lp of each
dc on hook, dc in next 2 sc, YO and draw
through all 3 lps on hook: cluster made; ch
5; rep from 18 times more *, YO, draw up
lp in next dc, YO, draw through 2 lps on
hook, insert hook in 3rd ch of beg ch-5, YO
and draw through same ch and through 2
lps on hook.

Rnd 12: Sl st in next ch-5 sp, ch 1, in same
sp and in each rem sp work (sc, hdc, 3 dc,
hdc, sc); join in first sc.

Finish off and weave in ends.

77

HIDDEN PINEAPPLES

Designed by Sandy Scoville

Time to make: About 1½ hours

SIZE:

5" x 5" square

MATERIALS:

Bedspread-weight crochet thread,
  150 yds cream
Size 7 (1.5 mm) steel crochet hook or size
  required for gauge

GAUGE:

8 dc = 1"

Instructions:

Ch 6, join to form a ring.

Rnd 1: Sl st in ring, ch 1, in ring work (3 sc, ch 3) 4 times; join in first sc: 12 sc.

Rnd 2: Ch 3 (counts as a dc on this and following rnds), dc in same sc, dc in next sc, 2 dc in next st, ch 5; * 2 dc in next sc, dc in next sc, 2 dc in next st, ch 5; rep from * twice more; join in 3rd ch of beg ch-3: 20 dc.

Rnd 3: Ch 4 (counts as a dc and a ch-1 sp), (dc in next dc, ch 1) 3 times; dc in next dc, ch 5, sk next ch-5 sp; * (dc in next dc, ch 1) 4 times; dc in next dc, ch 5, sk next ch-5 sp; rep from * twice more; join in 3rd ch of beg ch-4.

Rnd 4: Sl st in next ch-1 sp, ch 1, sc in same sp; (ch 3, sc in next ch-1 sp) 3 times; ch 5, sc in next ch-5 sp, ch 5; * sc in next ch-1 sp, (ch 3, sc in next ch-1 sp) 3 times; ch 5, sc in next ch-5 sp, ch 5; rep from * twice more; join.

Rnd 5: Sl st in first ch of next ch-3 sp, ch 1, sc in same sp; * † (ch 3, sc in next ch-3 sp) twice; ch 3, sc in 3rd ch of next ch-5 sp, ch 5, sc in 3rd ch of next ch-5 sp †; ch 3, sc in next ch-3 sp; rep from * twice more, then rep from † to † once; ch 3; join.

Rnd 6: Sl st in first ch of next ch-3 sp, ch 1, sc in same sp; * † ch 3, sc in next ch-3 sp, ch 3; sc in 2nd ch of next ch-3 sp, ch 3, 7 dc in next ch-5 sp; ch 3, sc in 2nd ch of next ch-3 sp, ch 3 †; sc in next ch-3 sp; rep from * twice more, then rep from † to † once; join.

Rnd 7: Sl st in first ch of next ch-3 sp, ch 1, sc in same sp; * † ch 7, sk next 2 ch-3 sps, dc in next dc, (ch 1, dc in next dc) 6 times; ch 7, sk next 2 ch-3 sps †; sc in next ch-3 sp; rep from * twice more, then rep from † to † once; join.

Rnd 8: Sl st in first 3 chs of next ch-7 sp, ch 1, sc in next ch; ch 5; * † sc in next ch-1 sp, (ch 3, sc in next ch-1 sp) 5 times; ch 5 †; (sc in 4th ch of next ch-7 sp, ch 5) twice; rep from * twice more, then rep from † to † once; sc in 4th ch of next ch-7 sp, ch 5; join.

Rnd 9: Sl st in first 2 chs of next ch-5 sp, ch 1, sc in next ch, ch 5; * † sc in next ch-3 sp, (ch 3, sc in next ch-3 sp) 4 times; ch 5, sc in 3rd ch of next ch-5 sp, ch 5, 5 sc in next ch-5 sp; ch 5,† sc in 3rd ch of next ch-5 sp, ch 5; rep from * twice more, then rep from † to † once; join.

Rnd 10: Sl st in first 2 chs of next ch-5 sp, ch 1, sc in next ch, ch 5; * † sc in next ch-3 sp, (ch 3, sc in next ch-3 sp) 3 times; ch 5, sc in 3rd ch of next ch-5 sp, ch 3, sc in 3rd ch of next ch-5 sp, ch 3, sc in next sc, (ch 3, sk next sc, sc in next sc) twice †; (ch 3, sc in 3rd ch of next ch-5 sp) twice; ch 5; rep from * twice more, then rep from † to † once; ch 3, sc in 3rd ch of next ch-5 sp, ch 3; join.

Rnd 11: Sl st in first 2 chs of next ch-5 sp, ch 1, sc in next ch; ch 5; * † sc in next ch-3 sp, (ch 3, sc in next ch-3 sp) twice; ch 5, sc in 3rd ch of next ch-5 sp, ch 5, sk next ch-3 sp, sc in next ch-3 sp, ch 5, sk next 2 ch-3 sps, sc in next ch-3 sp, ch 5, sk next ch-3 sp †; sc in 3rd ch of next ch-5 sp, ch 5; rep from * twice more, then rep from † to † once; join.

Rnd 12: Sl st in first 2 chs of next ch-5 sp, ch 1, sc in next ch, ch 5; * † sc in next ch-3 sp, ch 3, sc in next ch-3 sp, ch 5, sc in 3rd ch of next ch-5 sp, ch 3, 7 sc in each of next 3 ch-5 sps; ch 3 †; sc in 3rd ch of next ch-5 sp, ch 5; rep from * twice more, then rep from † to † once; join.

Rnd 13: Sl st in first 2 chs of next ch-5 sp, ch 1, sc in next ch, ch 5; * † keeping last lp of each tr on hook, 3 tr in next ch-3 sp, YO and draw through all 4 lps on hook: cluster made; ch 3, sl st in top of same cluster: picot made; ch 5, sc in 3rd ch of next ch-5 sp, ch 3, 5 sc in next ch-3 sp, working in BLs only, sc in next sc, (ch 3, sk next sc, sc in next sc) 3 times; sc in BL of next 7 sc, working in BLs only, sc in next sc, (ch 3, sk next sc, sc in next sc) 3 times, 5 sc in next ch-3 sp; ch 3 †; sc in 3rd ch of next ch-5 sp, ch 5; rep from * twice more, then rep from † to † once; join.

Finish off. Weave in ends.

DIAMONDS IN THE SQUARE

Designed by Sandy Scoville

Time to make: About 1 hour

SIZE:

4" x 4" square

MATERIALS:

Bedspread weight crochet thread,
    100 yds cream
Size 7 (1.5 mm) steel crochet hook or size
    required for gauge

GAUGE:

8 dc = 1"

Instructions:

Ch 4, join to form a ring.

Rnd 1: Ch 1, 8 sc in ring; join in first sc.

Rnd 2: Ch 1, working in BLs only, sc in same sc; ch 5, sk next sc, (sc in next sc, ch 5, sk next sc) 3 times; join: 4 ch-5 sps.

Rnd 3: Sl st in first ch of next ch-5 sp, ch 1, 6 sc in same sp and in each rem sp; join: 24 sc.

Rnd 4: Ch 1, working in BLs only, sc in same sc, ch 3, sk next sc, sc in next sc, ch 14, sk next sc, sc in next sc, ch 3, sk next sc; * sc in next sc, ch 3, sk next sc, sc in next sc, ch 14, sk next sc, sc in next sc, ch 3, sk next sc; rep from * twice more; join: 4 ch-14 sps.

Rnd 5: Sl st in first ch of next ch-3 sp, ch 1, sc in same sp; * † ch 3, sk first ch of next ch-14, dc in next 4 chs, 2 dc in each of next 2 chs, ch 3, 2 dc in each of next 2 chs, dc in next 4 chs, ch 3, sk next ch, sc in next ch-3 sp, ch 3 †; sc in next ch-3 sp; rep from * twice more, then rep from † to † once; join.

Rnd 6: Sl st in first ch of next ch-3 sp, ch 1, sc in same sp; * † ch 1, sc in next 8 dc, in next ch-3 sp work (sc, ch 5, sc); sc in next 8 dc, ch 1 †; draw up lp in each of next 3 ch-3 sps, YO and draw through all 4 lps on hook; rep from * twice more, then rep from † to † once; draw up lp in next 2 ch-3 sps and in first sc, YO and draw through all 4 lps on hook; join.

Rnd 7: Sl st in next ch-1 sp, ch 1, sc in same sp; * † working in BLs only, (ch 3, sk next sc, sc in next sc) 4 times; ch 7, sk next sc, next ch-5 sp, and next sc, (sc in next sc, ch 3, sk next sc) 4 times; sc in next ch-1 sp, ch 3 †; sc in next ch-1 sp; rep from * twice more, then rep from † to † once; join.

Rnd 8: Sl st in first ch of next ch-3 sp, ch 1, sc in same sp; * † ch 5, sk next ch-3 sp, sc in next ch-3 sp, ch 5, sk next ch-3 sp, in next ch 7 sp work (sc, ch 5, sc); ch 5, sk

next ch-3 sp, sc in next ch-3 sp, ch 5 †; sk next ch-3 sp, draw up lp in each of next 3 ch-3 sps, YO and draw through all 4 lps on hook; rep from * twice more, then rep from † to † once, draw up lp in each of next 2 ch-3 sps and in first sc, YO and draw through all 4 lps on hook; join.

Rnd 9: Sl st in first ch of next ch-5 sp, ch 1, in same sp work (sc, hdc, 2 dc, tr, 2 dc, hdc, sc): shell made; shell in next ch-5 sp; * † in next ch-5 sp work (sc, hdc, 2 dc, 3 tr, 2 dc, hdc sc): corner shell made †; shell in each of next 4 ch-5 sps;. rep from * twice more, then rep from † to † once; shell in next 2 ch-5 sps; join.

Finish off. Weave in ends.

PRETTY PINWHEEL

Designed by Sandy Scoville

Time to make: About 1 hour

SIZE:

4½" diameter

MATERIALS:

Bedspread weight crochet thread,
 100 yds cream
Size 7 (1.5 mm) steel crochet hook or size
 required for gauge

GAUGE:

8 dc = 1"

Instructions:

Ch 6, join to form a ring.

Rnd 1: Ch 1, 12 sc in ring; join in first sc.

Rnd 2: Ch 3 (counts as a dc on this and following rnds), dc in next sc; ch 3, (dc in next 2 sc, ch 3) 5 times; join in 3rd ch of beg ch-3: 6 ch-3 sps.

Rnd 3: Sl st in next dc and in first ch of next ch-3 sp, ch 1, in same sp work (sc, ch 3, sc); ch 5; * in next ch-3 sp work (sc, ch 3, sc); ch 5; rep from * around; join to first sc.

Rnd 4: Ch 1; * in next ch-3 sp work (sc, ch 3, sc); ch 3, 3 dc in next ch-5 sp, ch 3; rep from * around; join to first sc.

Rnd 5: Ch 1; * in next ch-3 sp work (sc, ch 3, sc); ch 3, 2 dc in next dc; ch 1, sk next dc, 2 dc in next dc; ch 3; rep from * around; join.

Rnd 6: Ch 1, * in next ch-3 sp work (sc, ch 3, sc); ch 3, 2 dc in next dc; ch 1, sk next dc, 2 dc in next ch-1 sp; ch 1, sk next dc, 2 dc in next dc; ch 3; rep from * around; join: 12 ch-1 sps.

Rnd 7: Ch 1; * in next ch-3 sp work (sc, ch 3, sc); ch 3, 2 dc in next dc; ch 1, sk next dc, 2 dc in next ch-1 sp; ch 1, sk next 2 dc, 2 dc in next ch-1 sp; ch 1, sk next dc, 2 dc in next dc; ch 3; rep from * around; join: 18 ch-1 sps.

Rnd 8: Ch 1; * in next ch-3 sp work (sc, ch 3, sc); ch 3, 2 dc in next dc; ch 1, sk next dc, 2 dc in next ch-1 sp; (ch 1, sk next 2 dc, 2 dc in next ch-1 sp) twice; ch 1, sk next dc, 2 dc in next dc; ch 3; rep from * around; join: 24 ch-1 sps.

Rnd 9: Ch 1; * in next ch-3 sp work (sc, ch 3, sc); ch 3, 2 dc in next dc; ch 1, sk next dc, 2 dc in next ch-1 sp; (ch 1, sk next 2 dc, 2 dc in next ch-1 sp) 3 times; ch 1, sk next dc, 2 dc in next dc; ch 3; rep from * around; join: 30 ch-1 sps.

Rnd 10: Ch 1, *in next ch-3 sp work (sc, ch 3, sc); ch 3, sc in next dc; (ch 3, sc in next dc, in next ch 1-sp, and in next dc) 5 times; ch 3, sc in next dc, ch 3; rep from * 5 times; ch 3, sc in next dc, ch 3; rep from * 5 times more; join in first sc.

Finish off. Weave in ends.

MUST HAVE BLOUSE

Designed by Denise Black

Note: *Instructions are written for size Small; changes for larger sizes are in parentheses.*

Size:	Small	Medium	Large
Body Chest Measurements:	30"–32"	34"–36"	38"–40"
Finished Chest Measurement:	36"	40"	44"

Time to make: About 14 hours

MATERIALS:

Sport weight yarn, 11 (13, 15) oz, aqua

Note: *Photographed model made with Patons® Astra, #2755 Blue Aqua.*

Size F (3.75 mm) crochet hook, or size required for gauge

Size 16 tapestry needle

GAUGE:

5 dc = 1"

Instructions:

BACK:

Ch 91 (101, 111).

Row 1 (right side)**:** Dc in 4th ch from hook (beg 3 skipped chs count as a dc) and in each rem ch: 89 (99, 109) dc. Ch 1, turn.

Row 2: Sl st in first dc, dc in next dc; * sl st in next dc, dc in next dc; rep from * to beg 3 skipped ch, sl st in 3rd ch of beg 3 skipped chs. Ch 3 (counts as a dc on following rows), turn.

Row 3: Dc in each dc and sl st. Ch 1, turn.

Row 4: Sl st in first dc, dc in next dc; * sl st in next dc, dc in next dc; rep from * to turning ch 3, sl st in 3rd ch of turning ch. Ch 3, turn.

Row 5: Dc in each st. Ch 1, turn.

Rep Rows 4 and 5 until piece measures

about 12" (12", 14") ending by working a right side row.

ARMHOLE SHAPING:

Row 1 (wrong side)**:** Sl st in first 10 (12, 12) sts; * dc in next dc, sl st in next dc; rep from * to last 8 (10, 10) dc and turning ch-3. Ch 3, turn, leaving rem dc and turning ch unworked.

Row 2 (right side)**:** Dc in each st to last 9 (11, 11) sl sts-71 (77, 87) sts. Ch 1, turn, leaving rem sl sts unworked.

Row 3: Sl st in first dc, dc in next dc; * sl st in next dc, dc in next dc; rep from * to turning ch-3, sl st in 3rd ch of turning ch. Ch 3, turn.

Row 4: Dc in each st. Ch 1, turn.

Row 5: Sl st in first dc, dc in next dc; * sl st

in next dc, dc in next dc; rep from * to turning ch-3, sl st in 3rd ch of turning ch. Ch 3, turn.

Rep Rows 4 and 5 until armhole measures about 7" (7½", 7½"), ending by working a wrong side row.

RIGHT NECK AND SHOULDER SHAPING:

Row 1 (right side)**:** Dc in next 19 (22, 26) sts, dec over next 2 sts, [to work dec: (YO, draw up lp in next 2 sts, YO, draw through 2 lps on hook) twice; YO and draw through all 3 lps on hook-dec made), leave rest of sts unworked: 21 (24, 28) dc. Ch 1, turn, leaving rem sts unworked.

Row 2: Sl st in first dc, dc in next dc; * sl in next dc, dc in next dc; rep from * to turning ch-3, sl st in 3rd ch of turning ch. Ch 3, turn.

81

continued on page 82

MUST HAVE BLOUSE
continued

Row 3: Dc in each st.

Rep Rows 2 and 3 until armhole measures about 8″ (8½″, 8½″) ending by working a right side row.

Finish off.

LEFT NECK AND SHOULDER SHAPING:

Row 1 (right side): Hold back with right side facing and last row worked at top; sk next 27 (27, 29) sts from right neck and shoulder shaping; join in next st, ch 2, dc in each st across: 21 (24, 28) dc. Ch 1, turn.

Row 2: Sl st in first dc, dc in next dc; * sl st in next dc, dc in next dc; rep from * to last dc; sl st in last dc. Ch 3, turn, leaving beg ch-2 unworked.

Row 3: Dc in each st across.

Rep Rows 2 and 3 until armhole measures about 8″ (8½″, 8½″) ending with a right side row.

Finish off.

FRONT:

Work same as Back to Armhole Shaping.

ARMHOLE SHAPING:

Row 1 (wrong side): Sl st in first 10 (12, 12) sts; * dc in next dc, sl st in next dc; rep from * to last 8 (10, 10) dc and turning ch-3: 71 (77, 87) dc. Ch 3, turn, leaving rem dc and turning ch unworked.

Row 2 (right side): Dc in each st to last 9 (11, 11) sl sts: 71 (77, 87) sts. Ch 1, turn, leaving rem sl sts unworked.

Row 3: Sl st in first dc, dc in next dc; * sl st in next dc, dc in next dc; rep from * to beg ch-3, sl st in 3rd ch of beg ch. Ch 3, turn.

Row 4: Dc in each st. Ch 1, turn.

Row 5: Sl st in first dc, dc in next dc; * sl st in next dc, dc in next dc; rep from * to turning ch-3, sl st in 3rd ch of turning ch. Ch 3, turn.

Rep Rows 4 and 5 until armhole measures about 5″ (5½″, 5½″), ending by working a wrong side row.

LEFT NECK AND SHOULDER SHAPING:

Row 1 (right side): Dc in next 19 (22, 26) sts; dec over next 2 sts twice [to work dec: (YO, draw up lp in next st, YO, draw through 2 lps on hook) twice; YO and draw through all 3 lps on hook: dec made]: 21 (24, 28) dc. Ch 1, turn, leaving rem sts unworked.

Row 2: Sl st in first dc, dc in next dc; * sl st in next dc, dc in next dc; rep from * to turning ch-3, sl st in 3rd ch of turning ch. Ch 3, turn.

Row 3: Dc in each st.

Rep Rows 2 and 3 until armhole measures about 8″ (8½″, 8½″) ending by working a right side row.

Finish off.

RIGHT NECK AND SHOULDER SHAPING:

Row 1 (right side): Hold back with right side facing and last row worked at top; sk next 27 (27, 29) sts from right neck and shoulder shaping; join in next st, ch 2, dc in each st across: 21 (24, 28) dc. Ch 1, turn.

Row 2: Sl st in first dc, dc in next dc; * sl st in next dc, dc in next dc; rep from * to last dc; sl st in last dc. Ch 3, turn, leaving beg ch-2 unworked.

Row 3: Dc in each st across.

Rep Rows 2 and 3 until armhole measures about 8 (8½″, 8½″) ending by working a right side row.

Finish off.

SLEEVE (MAKE 2):

Ch 67 (69, 69).

Row 1 (right side): Dc in 4th ch from hook and in each rem ch: 65 (67, 67) dc. Ch 1, turn.

Row 2: Sl st in first dc, dc in next dc; * sl st in next dc, dc in next dc; rep from * to beg 3 skipped ch, sl st in 3rd ch of beg 3 skipped ch. Ch 3, turn.

Row 3: 2 dc in first st, dc in each rem st to last st, 2 dc in last st: 67 (69, 69) dc. Ch 1, turn.

Row 4: Sl st in first dc, dc in next dc; * sl st in next dc, dc in next dc; rep from * to turning ch-3, sl st in 3rd ch of turning ch. Ch 3, turn.

Rows 5 through 14: Rep Rows 3 and 4 five times. At end of last row: 77 (79, 79) sts.

Row 15: Dc in each dc. Ch 1, turn.

Row 16: Sl st in first dc, dc in next dc; * sl st in next dc, dc in next dc; rep from * to turning ch-3, sl st in 3rd ch of turning ch. Ch 3, turn.

Rep Rows 15 and 16 until sleeve measures about 5½" (6", 6") ending by working a right side row. Finish off.

ASSEMBLY:
Sew shoulder seams. Sew sleeves to front and back having center of sleeves at shoulder seams. Sew sleeve and side seams. Weave in ends.

BOTTOM EDGING:
Hold sweater with right side facing and beg ch at top. Working in unused lps of beg ch, join yarn in one side seam; * ch 1, sl st in next lp; rep from * to joining, join. Finish off.

SLEEVE EDGING:
Hold sweater with right side facing and one sleeve edge at top; working in unused lps of beg ch of sleeve, join yarn in seam; * ch 1, sl st in next lp; rep from * to joining, join. Finish off. Weave in ends.

Repeat for other sleeve.

SUNSHINE BLOCKS

Designed by Denise Black

Time to make: About 13 hours

SIZE:
46" x 60"

MATERIALS:
Worsted weight yarn, 36 oz gold
*Note: Photographed model made
with Red Heart® Plush™,
#9220 Apricot Yellow*
Size H (5 mm) crochet hook, or size
required for gauge
Size 16 tapestry needle

GAUGE:
7 dc = 2"

PATTERN STITCH:
Puff Stitch (puff st): (YO, draw up lp in st
indicated) 5 times; YO and draw through all
11 lps on hook: puff st made. Push puff st
to right side.

Instructions:
Ch 170.

Row 1 (right side)**:** Dc in 4th ch from hook
(beg 3 skipped chs count as a dc), ch 2;
* sk next 2 chs, dc in next 7 chs, ch 2; rep
from * 17 times more; sk next 2 chs, dc in
next 2 chs: 130 dc. Ch 2 (counts as a dc on
following rows), turn.

Row 2: Dc in next dc, ch 2; * sk next ch-2
sp and next dc; 2 dc in next dc; ch 1, sk
next dc, puff st (see Pattern Stitch) in next

dc; ch 1, sk next dc, 2 dc in next dc; ch 2,
sk next dc; rep from * 17 times more; sk
next ch-2 sp, dc in next dc and in 3rd ch of
beg 3 skipped ch. Ch 2, turn.

Row 3: Dc in next dc; * ch 2, sk next ch-2
sp, dc in next 2 dc, dc in next ch-1 sp, dc in
next puff st, dc in next ch-1 sp, dc in next 2
dc; rep from * 17 times more; ch 2, sk next
ch-2 sp, dc in next dc and in 2nd ch of
turning ch-2. Ch 2, turn.

Row 4: Dc in next dc; * ch 2, sk next ch-2
sp, dc in next dc, (ch 1, sk next dc, dc in
next dc) 3 times; rep from * 17 times more;
ch 2, sk next ch-2 sp, dc in next dc and in
2nd ch of turning ch-2. Ch 2, turn.

Row 5: Dc in next dc; * ch 2, sk next ch-2
sp, dc in next dc, (dc in next ch-1 sp and in
next dc) 3 times; rep from * 17 times more;
ch 2, sk next ch-2 sp, dc in next dc and in
2nd ch of turning ch-2, ch 2, turn.

Row 6: Dc in next dc, ch 2; * sk next ch-2
sp and next dc; 2 dc in next dc; ch 1, sk
next dc, puff st in next dc; ch 1, sk next dc,
2 dc in next dc; ch 2, sk next dc; rep from
* 17 times more; sk next ch-2 sp, dc in
next dc and in 2nd ch of turning ch-2.
Ch 2, turn.

Row 7: Dc in next dc; * ch 2, sk next ch-2
sp, dc in next 2 dc, in next ch-1 sp, in next
puff st, in next ch-1 sp, and in next 2 dc;

rep from * 17 times more; ch 2, sk next ch-
2 sp, dc in next dc and in 2nd ch of turning
ch-2. Ch 2, turn.

Rep Rows 4 through 7 until afghan measures about 58" ending with a Row 7. At
end of last row do not ch 3, do not turn.
Finish off.

BOTTOM BORDER:
Hold afghan with right side facing and beg
ch at top, join in right hand corner in first
unused lp. Ch 3, dc in each unused lp of
beg ch across. Finish off. Weave in ends.

ABSOLUTELY PRECIOUS

Designed by Denise Black

Note: *Instructions are written for size 3 months; changes for larger size are in parentheses.*

Size:	3 months	6 months
Sweater - Finished Chest Measurement:	20"	22"
Hat - Finished Head Measurement:	15"	18"

Time to make: About 8 hours

MATERIALS:

Sport weight yarn, 6 (8) oz pink
Note: *Photographed model made with Bernat® Softee Baby #02001 Pink*
Size F (3.75 mm) crochet hook, or size required for gauge
Size 16 tapestry needle
3 buttons, ½" diameter
sewing needle and matching thread

GAUGE:

9 dc = 2"

HAT GAUGE:

First 3 rnds = 2½"

Sweater Instructions:

YOKE:

Starting at neckline, ch 43 (47).

Row 1: Dc in 4th ch from hook (beg 3 skipped chs counts as a dc), and in next 6 chs; in next ch work (2 dc, ch 2, 2 dc)-shell made; dc in next 2 (4) chs, in next ch work (2 dc, ch 2, 2 dc); dc in next 17 chs, in next ch work (2 dc, ch 2, 2 dc); dc in next 2 (4) chs, in next ch work (2 dc, ch 2, 2 dc); dc in next 8 chs; ch 3 (counts as dc on following rows), turn: 53 (57) dc and four shells.

Row 2: * Dc in each dc to ch-2 sp of next shell; shell in ch-2 sp; rep from * 3 times more; dc in each rem dc and in 3rd ch of beg 3 skipped chs. Ch 3, turn.

Row 3: * Dc in each dc to ch-2 sp of next shell; shell in ch-2 sp; rep from * 3 times more; dc in each rem dc and in 3rd ch of turning ch-3. Ch 3, turn: 85 (89) dc.

Rows 4 through 5 (6): Rep Row 3, at end of Row 5 (6): 117 (137) dc.

Row 6 (7): * Dc in each dc to ch-2 sp of next shell; in next ch-2 sp work (dc, ch 2, dc); rep from * 3 times more; dc in each rem dc and in 3rd ch of turning ch-3. Ch 3, turn: 125 (145) dc.

Rows 7 (8) through 9 (10): Rep Row 6 (7), at end of last row: 149 (169) dc.

BODY:

Row 1 (right side):
* Dc in each dc to ch-2 sp of next shell; † YO, insert hook in ch-2 sp; YO and pull up lp, YO and draw through 2 lps on hook †; sk next 30 (36) dc: armhole made; rep from † to † once; YO and draw though all 3 lps on hook; rep from * once more; dc in each rem dc and in 3rd ch of turning ch-3. Ch 3, turn: 91 (99) dc on body.

Row 2: Sc in first dc, dc in next dc; * sc in next dc, dc in next dc; rep from * to turning ch-3; sc in 3rd ch of turning ch. Ch 3, turn.

Row 3: * Sc in next dc, dc in next sc; rep from * across. Ch 1, turn.

Row 4: Sc in first dc, dc in next sc; * sc in next dc, dc in next sc; rep from * to turning ch-3; sc in 3rd ch of turning ch. Ch 3, turn.

Rep Rows 3 and 4 until piece measures about 5 (6)" from underarm. At end of last row do not ch 1. Finish off.

86

RIGHT SLEEVE:

Hold sweater with right side facing, and holding ch-2 sps of armholes with wrong sides together and working through both thicknesses at same time; join in ch-2 sp of last row of yoke at underarm.

Row 1 (right side)**:** Ch 2, dc in each dc around; sk beg ch-2; join in first dc: 30 (36) dc. Ch 1, turn.

Row 2: Sc in same ch as joining, dc in next st; * sc in next st, dc in next st; rep from * around; join in first sc. Ch 3 (counts as a dc on following rows), turn.

Row 3: Sc in next st; * dc in next st, sc in next st; rep from * around; join in 3rd ch of turning ch-3. Ch 1, turn.

Rep Rows 2 and 3 until piece measure 6 (6½)" from underarm, ending by working a right side row. At end of last row ch 1, do not turn.

EDGING:

Rnd 1 (right side)**:** Sc in same ch as joining and in next st; dec over next 2 sts (to work dec: draw up lp in each of next 2 sts, YO and draw through all 3 lps on hook-dec made); * sc in next 2 sts, dec over next 2 sts; rep from * around; join in first sc.

Rnd 2: Ch 1, sl st in next st; * ch 1, sl st in next st; rep from * around; join in first sl st. Finish off.

Repeat for Left sleeve.

SWEATER EDGING:

Hold sweater with right side facing and bottom edge at top; join in first st in upper right hand corner.

Rnd 1 (right side)**:** Ch 1, sc in same st as joining and in each st across bottom edge; working along right front edge in ends of rows, 2 sc in first row, sc in each row to Row 1 of Body; 2 sc in each row to neck

edge; 3 sc in first st of right neck edge, sc in each st along right neck, along back, in each st along left neck to last st, 3 sc in last st; working along left front in ends of rows, 2 sc in each row through Row 1 of body; sc in each row to last row, 2 sc in last row, join in first sc.

Rnd 2: * Ch 1, sl st in next sc; rep from * around; join in first sl st.

Finish off. Weave in ends.

HAT:

Ch 4.

Rnd 1 (right side)**:** 11 dc in 4th ch from hook (beg 3 skipped chs count as a dc); join in 3rd ch of beg 3 skipped chs: 12 dc.

Rnd 2: Ch 3 (counts as a dc on this and following rnds), 2 dc in each rem dc; join: 24 dc.

Rnd 3: Ch 3, dc in same ch as joining; dc in next dc, * 2 dc in next dc, dc in next dc; rep from * around; join: 36 dc.

Rnd 4: Ch 3, dc in same ch as joining; dc in next 2 dc, * 2 dc in next dc, dc in next 2 dc; rep from * around; join: 48 dc.

Rnd 5: Ch 3, dc in same ch as joining; dc in next 3 dc, * 2 dc in next dc, dc in next 3 dc; rep from * around; join: 60 dc.

For Size 6 months only:

Rnd 6: Ch 3, dc in same ch as joining; dc in next 4 dc, * 2 dc in next dc, dc in next 4 dc; rep from * around; join: 72 dc.

For both sizes:

Rnd 6 (7): Ch 3, dc in each dc; join in 3rd ch of beg ch-3: 60 (72) dc.

Rnd 7 (8): Rep Rnd 6 (7).

Note: Remaining rnds are working in joined rows and turned.

Rnd 8 (9): Ch 1, sc in same ch, dc in next dc; * sc in next dc, dc in next dc; rep from * around; join in first sc. Ch 3 (counts as a dc on following rnds), turn.

Rnd 9 (10): Sc in next dc; * dc in next sc, sc in next dc; join. Ch 1, turn.

Rnd 10 (11): Sc in same ch as joining, dc in next sc, * sc in next dc, dc in next sc; rep from * around; join in first sc. Ch 3, turn.

Rnd 11 (12): Sc in next dc; * dc in next sc, sc in next dc; rep from * around. Ch 1, turn.

Rnds 12 (13) through 15 (16): Rep Rnds 10 (11) and 11 (12) twice more.

Rnd 16 (17): Rep Rnd 10 (11), at end of rnd do not ch-3, do not turn.

Rnd 17 (18): * Ch 1, sl st in next st; rep from * around; join in joining.

Finish off. Weave in ends.

BABY DREAMS

Designed by Denise Black

Time to make: About 14 hours

SIZE:
36" x 42"

MATERIALS:
Sport weight yarn, 23 oz, blue
Note: *Photographed model made with Patons® Astra, #2774 Medium Blue*
Size G (4 mm) crochet hook, or size required for gauge
Size 16 tapestry needle

GAUGE:
In pattern 3 shells = 5"

Instructions
Ch 141.

Row 1 (right side)**:** Sc in 2nd ch from hook and in each ch: 140 sc. Ch 1, turn.

Row 2: Sc in first sc, (ch 3, sk next 2 sc, sc in next sc) twice; * ch 3, sc in next sc, (ch 3, sk next 2 sc, sc in next sc) twice; rep from * 18 times more: 60 sc and 59 ch-3 sps. Ch 2 (counts as first dc on following rows), turn.

Row 3: 3 dc in next ch-3 sp; sc in next sc; * sk next ch-3 sp, in next ch-3 sp work (3 dc, ch 3, 3 dc): shell made; sk next sc and next ch-3 sp, sc in next sc; rep from * 18 times more; 3 dc in next ch-3 sp; dc in next sc: 19 shells. Ch 1, turn.

Row 4: Sc in first dc, ch 3, sk next 3 dc, in next sc work (sc, ch 3, sc): V-st made; * ch 3, sc in ch-3 sp of next shell, ch 3, sk next 3 dc of same shell, in next sc work (sc, ch 3, sc): V-st made; rep from * 18 times more; ch 3, sk next 3 dc, sc in 2nd ch of turning ch-2. Ch 1, turn.

Row 5: Sc in first sc, * sk next ch-3 sp, in ch-3 sp of next V-st work shell; sk next sc and next ch-3 sp, sc in next sc; rep from * 19 times more. Ch 1, turn.

Row 6: Sc in first sc, ch 3, sc in ch-3 sp of next shell, ch 3; * in next sc work V-st; ch 3, sc in ch-3 sp of next shell, ch 3; rep from * 18 times more; sc in next sc. Ch 2, turn.

Row 7: 3 dc in next ch-3 sp; sc in next sc; * sk next ch-3 sp, in next ch-3 sp of next V-st work shell; sk next ch-3 sp, sc in next sc; rep from * 18 times more; 3 dc in next ch-3 sp, dc in next sc. Ch 1, turn.

Rows 8 through 103: Rep Rows 4 through 7, 24 times more.

Rows 104 through 106: Rep Rows 4 through 6. Do not finish off; ch 2, turn.

BORDER:
Rnd 1: Working across last row, 3 dc in next ch-3 sp; sc in next sc; (sk next ch-3 sp, in next ch-3 sp of next V-st work shell; sk next ch-3 sp, sc in next sc); 19 times; 3 dc in next ch-3 sp, dc in next sc, ch 1, working along next side in ends of rows; sc in next 2 rows, sk next 2 rows, shell in next row, sk next 2 rows; (sc in next row, sk next 2 rows, shell in next row, sk next 2 rows) 16 times; sc in next 2 rows; sk next row, working along bottom edge in unused lps of beg ch, sc in next 4 lps, sk next 3 lps, shell in next lp; sk next 2 lps; (sc in next lp, sk next 3 lps, shell in next lp, sk next 2 lps) 18 times; sc in next 4 lps; working along next edge in ends of rows, sk first row, sc in next 2 rows, sk next 2 rows, shell in next row; sk next 2 rows; (sc in next row, sk next 2 rows, shell in next row, sk next 2 rows) 16 times; sc in next 2 rows, join in 2nd ch of turning ch-2.

Rnd 2: Ch 1, sc in same ch as joining and in next 3 sc; † (sc in next 3 dc, 3 sc in next ch-3 sp, sc in next 3 dc, sk next sc)18 times; sc in next 3 dc, 3 sc in next ch-3 sp, sc in next 3 dc, sc in next 6 sc; (sc in next 3 dc, 3 sc in next ch-3 sp, sc in next 3 dc, sk next sc) 16 times; sc in next 3 dc, 3 sc in next ch-3 sp, sc in next 3 dc †; sc in next 6 sc; rep from † to † once; sc in next 2 sc; join in first sc. Finish off. Weave in ends.

HELMET HAT WARDROBE

Designed by Sandy Scoville

CHILD'S HELMET HAT
PAGE 90

MOM'S HELMET HAT
PAGE 92

DAD'S HELMET HAT
PAGE 94

CHILD'S HELMET HAT

Time to make: 6 hours

SIZE:

18" circumference

MATERIALS:

Worsted weight yarn, 135 yds each
    mauve, red, off white, and navy;
    70 yds green
Size G (4 mm) crochet hook, or size
    required for gauge
Size H (5 mm) crochet hook
Size 16 tapestry needle

GAUGE:

4 sc = 1"

PATTERN STITCH:

Popcorn (PC): 4 dc in st indicated; remove hook from lp, insert hook in first dc made, draw dropped lp through, pull tight to form popcorn; ch 1: PC made.

Instructions:

With smaller size hook and green, ch 72, join to form a ring.

Rnd 1: Ch 1, sc in same ch as joining and in each rem ch; join in first sc: 72 sc.

Rnds 2 and 3: Ch 1, sc in same sc as joining and in each rem sc; join. At end of Rnd 3, drop green on wrong side of work; do not cut.

Rnd 4: Join mauve in same sc as joining, ch 1, sc in same sc and in next 2 sc; PC in next sc (see Pattern Stitch); * sc in next 3 sc, PC in next sc; rep from * around; join-18 PC. Cut mauve.

Rnd 5: With green, working over mauve, insert hook in 2nd sc of next 3-sc group on 2nd rnd below, ch 1, drawing up each lp to working row, work 3 sc in same sc on 2nd rnd below: 3 long sc made; sc in ch-1 sp of next PC; * 3 long sc in 2nd sc of next 3-sc

group on 2nd rnd below; sc in ch-1 sp of next PC; rep from * around; join.

Rnds 6 and 7: Ch 1, sc in same sc as joining and in each rem sc; join. At end of Rnd 7: 72 sc. Cut green.

Rnd 8: Join red in same sc as joining; ch 2 (counts as first hdc on this and following rnds), hdc in next sc and in each rem sc; join in 2nd ch of beg ch-2.

Change to larger size hook.

Rnd 9: With larger size hook, sl st in each hdc; join in first sl st. Cut red.

Rnd 10: Join off white in 2nd ch of beg ch-2 of Rnd 8; working behind sl sts on Rnd 9, sl st in each hdc on Rnd 8; join. (See diagram on page 91.)

Rnd 11: Ch 1, working behind sl sts on Rnds 9 and 10, sc in beg ch-2 on Rnd 8 (where already worked), sc in BL of each hdc on Rnd 8; join in first sc.

Rnd 12: Sl st in each sc; join in first sl st. Drop off-white on wrong side of work. Do not cut.

Rnd 13: Join navy in first sc on Rnd 11 behind sl sts on Rnd 12, working behind sl sts on Rnd 12, sl st in each rem sc on Rnd 11; join. Cut navy.

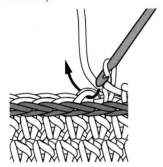

Working behind sl sts

Rnd 14: With off-white, sl st in each sc on Rnd 11 behind sl sts on Rnds 12 and 13; join.

Rnd 15: Ch 1, sc in each sc on Rnd 11 behind sl sts on Rnds 12, 13, and 14; join. Cut off-white.

Rnd 16: Join red in bump on back of same sc as joining, ch 1, sc in same sp and in bump on back of each rem sc; join.

Rnd 17: Ch 2, hdc in bump on back of next sc and in bump of back of each rem sc; join in 2nd ch of beg ch-2. Drop red on wrong side of work. Do not cut.

Change to smaller size hook.

Rnd 18: With smaller size hook, join green in 2nd ch of beg ch-2, ch 1, sc in same ch and in each hdc; join in first sc.

Rnd 19: Ch 1, sc in same sc as joining and in each sc; join. Drop green on wrong side of work. Do not cut.

Rnd 20: With red, rep Rnd 4. Cut red.

Rnds 21 and 22: With green, rep Rnds 5 and 6. At end of Rnd 22, cut green.

Rnd 23: Join mauve in BL of same sc as joining; ch 1, sc in same lp and in BL of each rem sc; join.

Rnd 24: Ch 2, hdc in BL of next 5 sc, dec over next 2 sc [to work dec: (YO, draw up lp in BL of next sc) twice; YO and draw through all 5 lps on hook: dec made]; * hdc in BL of next 6 sc, dec over next 2 sc; rep from

* around; join in 2nd ch of beg ch-2: 63 sts.

Rnd 25: Ch 1, sc in same ch as joining and in BL of each hdc; join in first sc. Cut mauve.

Rnd 26: Join navy in BL of same sc as joining, ch 1, sc in same lp and in BL of each rem sc; join.

Rnd 27: Ch 1, sc in same sc as joining; sc dec over next 2 sc (to work sc dec: draw up lp in each of next 2 sc, YO and draw through all 3 lps on hook: sc dec made); * sc in next sc, sc dec over next 2 sc; rep from * around; join: 42 sts.

Rnd 28: Ch 1, sc in same sc as joining; sc dec over next 2 sc; * sc in next sc, sc dec over next 2 sc; rep from * around; join: 28 sc.

Rnd 29: Ch 1, sc in same sc as joining; * sc dec over next 2 sc, sc in next sc; rep from * around; join: 19 sc.

Rnd 30: Ch 1, sc in same sc as joining; (sc dec) 9 times; join: 10 sc.

Rnd 31: Ch 1, sc dec over same sc as joining and next sc; (sc dec) 4 times; join: 5 sc.

Finish off, leaving a 6" end.

Thread end into tapestry needle; thread end through rem 5 sts and draw tight.

Weave in ends.

EAR FLAPS:
Right Ear Flap:
Hold hat with right side facing and beg ch at top; with smaller size hook, join green in 11th unused lp of beg ch to left of joining.

Row 1 (right side)**:** Ch 1, sc in same lp as joining; working in unused lps of beg ch, hdc in next 14 lps, sc in next lp: 16 sts. Ch 1, turn, leaving rem sts unworked.

Row 2: Sc in first sc, hdc in next 14 hdc, sc in next sc. Ch 1, turn.

Row 3: Sk first sc, sc in next hdc, hdc in next 12 hdc, sc in next hdc: 14 sts. Ch 1, turn, leaving rem sc unworked.

Row 4: Sc in first sc, hdc in next 12 hdc; sc in next sc. Ch 1, turn.

Row 5: Sk first sc, sc in next hdc, hdc in next 10 hdc, sc in next hdc: 12 sts. Ch 1, turn, leaving rem sc unworked.

Row 6: Sk first sc, sc in next hdc, hdc in next 8 hdc, sc in next hdc: 10 sts. Ch 1, turn, leaving rem sc unworked.

Row 7: Sk first sc, sc in next hdc, hdc in next 6 hdc, sc in next hdc: 8 sts. Ch 1, turn, leaving rem sc unworked.

Row 8: Sk first sc, sc in next hdc, hdc in next 4 hdc, sc in next hdc: 6 sts. Finish off, leaving rem sc unworked.

Left Ear Flap:
Sk next 20 unused lps on beg ch, join green in next lp.

Rows 1 through 8: Rep Rows 1 through 8 of right ear flap.

EDGING AND TIES:
Hold hat with right side of center back joining facing and lower edge at top; join green in same sc as joining; Ch 1, sc in same sc as joining and in each sc to right ear flap; * sc in side of each row of flap and in first 3 sts on last row; ch 60, sl st in second ch from hook and in each rem ch: tie made; sc in next 3 sts on last row and in side of each row of flap *; sc in each unused lp to left ear flap; rep from * to * once; sc in each rem unused lp; join in first sc.

Finish off. Weave in ends.

TASSEL:
Cut 22 strands of green 13" long. Lay 20 strands over center of one stand; tie 20 strands together tightly; pinch strands about 1" below tie, and wrap rem stand tightly around pinched strands; tie; hide ends. Using ends of tie at top of tassel, attach to top of hat. Trim ends.

MOM'S HELMET HAT

Designed by Sandy Scoville

Time to make: 6 hours 30 minutes

SIZE:

21" circumference

MATERIALS:

Worsted weight yarn, 35 yds each mauve, red, off-white, green, and navy; 70 yds, blue

Size G (4 mm) crochet hook, or size required for gauge

Size H (5 mm) crochet hook

Size 16 tapestry needle

GAUGE:

4 sc = 1"

PATTERN STITCH:

Popcorn (PC): 4 dc in st indicated; remove hook from lp, insert hook in first dc made, draw dropped lp through, pull tight to form popcorn; ch 1; PC made.

Instructions:

With smaller size hook and blue, ch 84, join to form a ring.

Rnd 1: Ch 1, sc in same ch as joining and in each rem ch; join in first sc: 84 sc.

Rnds 2 and 3: Ch 1, sc in same sc as joining and in each rem sc; join. At end of Rnd 3, drop blue on wrong side of work; do not cut.

Rnd 4: Join red in same sc as joining, ch 1, sc in same sc and in next 2 sc; PC in next sc (see Pattern Stitch); * sc in next 3 sc, PC in next sc; rep from * around; join: 21 PC. Cut red.

Rnd 5: With blue, working over red, insert hook in 2nd sc of next 3-sc group on 2nd rnd below, ch 1, drawing up each lp to working row, work 3 sc in same sc on 2nd rnd below: 3 long sc made; sc in ch-1 sp of next PC; * 3 long sc in 2nd sc of next 3-sc group on 2nd rnd below; sc in ch-1 sp of next PC; rep from * around; join.

Rnds 6 and 7: Ch 1, sc in same sc as joining and in each rem sc; join. At end of Rnd 7, cut blue.

Change to larger size hook.

Rnd 8: With larger size hook, join mauve in same sc as joining; sl st in each sc; join.

Rnd 9: Ch 1, working in sc on Rnd 7 behind Rnd 8, (see diagram on page 93) sc in first sc and in each rem sc; join. Cut mauve.

Rnd 10: Join green in bump on back of first sc, ch 1, sc in same sp and in bump on back of each rem sc; join. Drop green on wrong side of work.

92

Rnd 11: Join off-white in bump on back of first sc, ch 2 (counts as an hdc on this and following rnds), hdc in bump on back of each rem sc; join in 2nd ch of beg ch-2. Cut white.

Rnd 12: With green, sl st in same ch as joining and in each hdc; join.

Rnd 13: Ch 1, working in hdc on Rnd 11 behind Rnd 12, sc in beg ch-2 and in each hdc; join. Cut green.

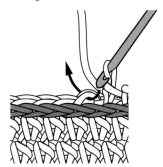

Working behind sl sts

Rnd 14: Join mauve in first sc; sl st in each sc; join.

Rnd 15: Ch 1, working in sc on Rnd 13 behind Rnd 14, sc in first sc and in each rem sc; join. Cut mauve.

Change to smaller size hook.

Rnd 16: With smaller size hook, join blue in bump on back of first sc, ch 1, sc in same sp and in bump on back of each rem sc; join.

Rnds 17 and 18: Ch 1, sc in same sc and in each rem sc; join. At end of Rnd 18, drop blue on wrong side of work. Do not cut.

Rnd 19: With navy, rep Rnd 4. Cut navy.

Rnds 20 through 22: With blue, rep Rnds 5 through 7. At end of Rnd 22, cut blue.

Rnd 23: Join red in BL of same sc as joining; ch 1, sc in same lp and in BL of each rem sc; join.

Rnd 24: Ch 2, hdc in BL of next 4 sc, dec over next 2 sc [to work dec: (YO, draw up lp in BL of next sc) twice; YO and draw through all 5 lps on hook: dec made]; * hdc in BL of next 5 sc, dec over next 2 sc; rep from * around; join in 2nd ch of beg ch-2: 72 sts.

Rnd 25: Ch 1, sc in same ch as joining and in BL of each hdc; join in first sc. Cut red.

Rnd 26: Join green in BL of same sc as joining, ch 1, sc in same lp and in BL of each

rem sc; join.

Rnd 27: Ch 1, sc in same sc as joining; sc dec over next 2 sc 9 (to work sc dec: draw up lp in each of next 2 sc, YO and draw through all 3 lps on hook: sc dec made); * sc in next sc, sc dec over next 2 sc; rep from * around; join: 48 sts.

Rnd 28: Ch 1, sc in same sc as joining; sc dec over next 2 sc; * sc in next sc, sc dec over next 2 sc; rep from * around; join: 32 sc.

Rnd 29: Ch 1, sc dec over same sc as joining and next sc; * sc in next sc, sc dec over next 2 sc; rep from * around; join: 21 sc.

Rnd 30: Ch 1, sc in same sc as joining; sc dec over next 2 sc; * sc in next sc, sc dec over next 2 sc; rep from * around; join: 14 sc.

Rnd 31: Ch 1, sc dec in same sc as joining and in next sc; (sc dec) 6 times; join: 7 sc.

Rnd 32: Ch 1, sc in same sc as joining; (sc dec) 3 times; join: 4 sc.

Finish off, leaving a 6″ end.

Thread end into tapestry needle; thread end through rem 4 sts and draw tight.

Weave in ends.

EAR FLAPS
Right Ear Flap:
Hold hat with right side facing and beg ch at top; with smaller size hook, join blue in 12th unused lp of beg ch to left of joining.

Row 1 (right side)**:** Ch 1, sc in same lp as joining; working in unused lps of beg ch, hdc in next 18 lps, sc in next lp: 20 sts. Ch 1, turn, leaving rem sts unworked.

Row 2: Sk first sc, sc in next hdc, hdc in next 16 hdc, sc in next hdc: 18 sts. Ch 1, turn, leaving rem sc unworked.

Row 3: Sk first sc, sc in next hdc, hdc in next 14 hdc, sc in next hdc: 16 sts. Ch 1, turn, leaving rem sc unworked.

Row 4: Sk first sc, sc in next hdc, hdc in next 12 hdc, sc in next hdc: 14 sts. Ch 1, turn, leaving rem sc unworked.

Row 5: Sk first sc, sc in next hdc, hdc in next 10 hdc, sc in next hdc: 12 sts. Turn, leaving rem sc unworked.

Row 6: Sk first sc, sc in next hdc, hdc in next 8 hdc, sc in next hdc: 10 sts. Ch 1,

turn, leaving rem sc unworked.

Row 7: Sk first sc, sc in next hdc, hdc in next 6 hdc, sc in next hdc: 8 sts. Ch 1, turn, leaving rem sc unworked.

Row 8: Sk first sc, sc in next hdc, hdc in next 4 hdc, sc in next hdc: 6 sts. Finish off.

Left Ear Flap:
Sk next 22 unused lps on beg ch, join blue in next lp.

Rows 1 through 8: Rep Rows 1 through 8 of right ear flap.

EDGING AND TIES:
Hold hat with right side of center back joining facing you and lower edge at top; with smaller size hook, join blue in same sc as joining; sc in each sc to right ear flap; * sc in side of each row of flap and in first 3 sts on last row; ch 65, sl st in second ch from hook and in each rem ch: tie made; sc in next 3 sts on last row and in side of each row of flap *; sc in each unused lp to left ear flap; rep from * to * once; sc in each rem unused lp; join in first sc.

Finish off. Weave in ends.

TASSEL:
Cut 22 strands of mauve 13″ long. Lay 20 strands over center of one stand; tie 20 strands together tightly; pinch strands about 1″ below tie, and wrap remaining strand tightly around pinched strands; tie; hide ends. Using ends of tie at top of tassel, attach to top of hat. Trim ends.

DAD'S HELMET HAT

Designed by Sandy Scoville

Time to make: 7 hours

SIZE:

22" circumference

MATERIALS:

Worsted weight yarn, 35 yds each mauve, off-white, green, blue, and navy; 140 yds red

Size G (4 mm) crochet hook, or size required for gauge

Size H (5 mm) crochet hook

Size 16 tapestry needle

GAUGE:

4 sc = 1"

PATTERN STITCH:

Popcorn (PC): 4 dc in st indicated; remove hook from lp, insert hook in first dc made, draw dropped lp through, pull tight to form popcorn; ch 1; PC made.

Instructions:

With smaller size hook and red, ch 88, join to form a ring.

Rnd 1: Ch 1, sc in same ch as joining and in each rem ch; join in first sc: 88 sc.

Rnds 2 and 3: Ch 1, sc in same sc as joining and in each rem sc; join. At end of Rnd 3, drop red on wrong side of work; do not cut.

Rnd 4: Join navy in same sc as joining, ch 1, sc in same sc and in next 2 sc; PC in next sc (see Pattern Stitch); * sc in next 3 sc, PC in next sc; rep from * around; join: 22 PC. Cut navy.

Rnd 5: With red, working over navy, insert hook in 2nd sc of next 3-sc group on 2nd rnd below, ch 1, drawing up each lp to working row, work 3 sc in same sc on 2nd rnd below: 3 long sc made; sc in ch-1 sp of next PC; * 3 long sc in 2nd sc of next 3-sc group on 2nd rnd below; sc in ch-1 sp of next PC; rep from * around; join.

Rnds 6 and 7: Ch 1, sc in same sc as joining and in each rem sc; join. At end of Rnd 7, cut red.

Change to larger size hook.

Rnd 8: With larger size hook, join off-white in same sc as joining; sl st in each sc; join.

Rnd 9: Ch 1, working in sc on Rnd 7 behind Rnd 8 (see diagram on page 95), sc in first sc and in each rem sc; join. Cut white.

Rnd 10: Join green in bump on back of first sc, ch 1, sc in same sp and in bump on back of each rem sc; join. Drop green on wrong side of work. Do not cut.

Rnd 11: Join mauve in back of first sc, ch 2 (counts as an hdc on this and following rnds), hdc in back of each sc; join in 2nd ch of beg ch-2. Cut mauve.

Rnd 12: With green, sl st in same ch as joining and in each hdc; join.

Rnd 13: Ch 1, working in hdc on Rnd 11 behind Rnd 12, sc in beg ch-2 and in each hdc; join. Cut green.

Rnd 14: Join off-white in first sc; sl st in each sc; join.

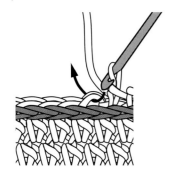

Working behind sl sts

Rnd 15: Ch 1, working in sc on Rnd 13 behind Rnd 14, sc in first sc and in each rem sc; join. Cut white.

Change to smaller size hook.

Rnd 16: With smaller size hook, join red in bump on back of first sc, ch 1, sc in same sp and in bump on back of each rem sc; join.

Rnds 17 and 18: Ch 1, sc in same sc and in each rem sc; join. At end of Rnd 18, drop red on wrong side of work. Do not cut.

Rnd 19: With blue, rep Rnd 4. Cut blue.

Rnds 20 through 22: With red, rep Rnds 5 through 7. At end of Rnd 22, cut red.

Rnd 23: Join green in BL of same sc as joining; ch 1, sc in same lp and in BL of each rem sc; join.

Rnd 24: Ch 2, hdc in BL of next 5 sc, dec over next 2 sc [to work dec: (YO, draw up lp in BL of next sc) twice; YO and draw through all 5 lps on hook: dec made]; * hdc in BL of next 6 sc, dec over next 2 sc; rep from * around; join in 2nd ch of beg ch-2: 77 sts.

Rnd 25: Ch 1, sc in same ch as joining and in BL of each hdc; join in first sc. Cut green.

Rnd 26: Join navy in BL of same sc as joining, ch 1, sc in same lp and in BL of each rem sc; join.

Rnd 27: Ch 1, sc in first 2 sc; sc dec over next 2 sc (to work sc dec: draw up lp in each of next 2 sc, YO and draw through all 3 lps on hook: sc dec made); sc in next sc; * dec over next 2 sc, sc in next sc; rep from * 23 times more: 52 sts.

Rnd 28: Ch 1, sc in same sc as joining; * sc dec over next 2 sc; sc in next sc; rep from * around; join: 35 sc.

Rnd 29: Ch 1, sc dec over same sc as joining and next sc; * sc in next sc, sc dec over next 2 sc; rep from * around; join: 23 sc. Cut navy.

Rnd 30: Join red in first sc; ch 1, sc dec over same sc as joining and next sc; * sc in next sc, sc dec over next 2 sc; rep from * around; join: 15 sc.

Rnd 31: Ch 1, sc in same sc as joining; sc dec over next 2 sc; * sc in next sc, sc dec over next 2 sc; join: 10 sc.

Rnd 32: Ch 1, sc in same sc as joining; * sc dec over next 2 sc; sc in next sc; rep from * around; join: 7 sc.

Rnd 33: Ch 1, sc in same sc as joining; (sc dec) 3 times; join in first sc: 4 sts.

Finish off, leaving a 6" end.

Thread end into tapestry needle; thread end through rem 4 sts and draw tight.

Weave in ends.

FLAP

Hold hat with right side facing and beg ch at top; with smaller size hook, join red in 32nd unused lp of beg ch to right of joining.

Row 1 (right side): Ch 1, sc in same lp as joining; working in unused lps of beg ch, hdc in next 62 lps, sc in next lp: 64 sts. Ch 1, turn, leaving rem sts unworked.

Row 2: Sk first sc, sc in next hdc, hdc in next 60 hdc, sc in next hdc: 62 sts. Ch 1, turn, leaving rem sc unworked.

Row 3: Sk first sc, sc in next hdc, hdc in next 58 hdc, sc in next hdc: 60 sts. Ch 1,

turn, leaving rem sc unworked.

Row 4: Sk first sc, sc in next hdc, hdc in next 56 hdc, sc in next hdc: 58 sts. Ch 1, turn, leaving rem sc unworked.

Row 5: Sk first sc, sc in next hdc, hdc in next 54 hdc, sc in next hdc: 56 sts. Ch 1, turn, leaving rem sc unworked.

Row 6: Sk first sc, sc in next hdc, hdc in next 52 hdc, sc in next hdc: 54 sts. Ch 1, turn, leaving rem sc unworked.

Row 7: Sk first sc, sc in next hdc, hdc in next 50 hdc, sc in next hdc: 52 sts. Ch 1, turn, leaving rem sc unworked.

Row 8: Sk first sc, sc in next hdc, hdc in next 48 hdc, sc in next hdc: 50 sts. Ch 1, turn, leaving rem sc unworked.

EDGING:

Sc in first sc, in each st along flap, in side of each row of flap, in each st along center front, and in side of each row of flap; join in first sc.

Finish off. Weave in ends.

Note: *Hat can be worn with Flap turned up, or turned down to protect ears and neck.*

KEYHOLE SCARF

Designed by Carol Mansfield

Time to Make: About 5 hours

SIZE:
67" x 5½"

MATERIALS:
Worsted weight yarn, 6 oz. red, 3 oz. blue
Note: *Photographed model made with Red Heart® Plush™ #9907 Red and #9851 Navy*
Size I (5.5 mm) aluminum crochet hook or size required for gauge.

Instructions:
With red, ch 21.

Row 1: Dc in 3rd ch from hook and in each rem ch: 19 dc; ch 2, turn.

Rows 2 through 20: Rep Row 1. In last st of Row 20, change to blue, ch 1, turn.

Row 21: Sc in each dc, ch 1, turn.

Row 22: Sc in each sc, ch 1, turn.

Row 23: Sc in each sc, change to red in last st, ch 2, turn.

Continue, working rows as follows:

15 rows red dc

3 rows blue sc

10 rows red dc

2 rows blue sc

6 rows red dc

2 rows blue sc

6 rows red dc

1 row blue sc (this is the center of scarf)

6 rows red dc

2 rows blue sc

6 rows red dc

2 rows blue sc

10 rows red dc

3 rows blue sc

15 rows red dc

3 rows blue sc

20 rows red dc

Finish off. Weave in ends.

FINISHING:
Following diagram, sew or sc scarf together.

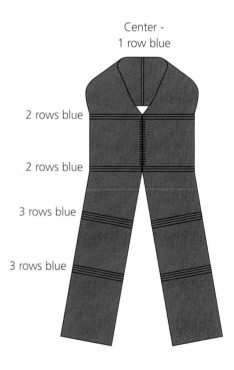

Center -
1 row blue

2 rows blue

2 rows blue

3 rows blue

3 rows blue

96

AROUND THE BLOCK AFGHAN

Designed by Sandy Scoville

Time to make: 23 hours 55 minutes

SIZE:
50" x 50" square

MATERIALS:
Worsted weight yarn, 3½ oz each, Colors A (Navy), B (Red), C (Medium Blue), and D (Coral), 7 oz each Colors E (Light Tan), F (Lavender), G (Dark Rust), H (Light Blue), and I (Red), and MC (Off-White) (trim)
Size I (5.5 mm) crochet hook, or size required for gauge
Size 16 tapestry needle

GAUGE:
3 dc = 1"

Instructions:
Beginning at center with Color A, ch 4, join to form a ring.

Rnd 1: Ch 3 (counts as a dc on this and following rnds), 3 dc in ring; ch 1, (4 dc in ring, ch 1) 3 times; join in 3rd ch of beg ch-3: 12 dec and 4 ch-1 sps.

Rnd 2: Sl st in next 3 dc and in next ch-1 sp, ch 3, in same sp work (3 dc, ch 1, 4 dc): beg corner made; ch 1; * in next ch-1 sp work (4 dc, ch 1, 4 dc): corner made; ch 1; rep from * twice more; join. Cut Color A. Finish off.

Rnd 3: Join MC in any corner ch-1 sp, ch 1, 3 sc in same sp; sc in each dc and in each ch-1 sp to next corner; * 3 sc in corner ch-1 sp; sc in each dc and in each ch-1 sp to next corner; rep from * twice more; join in first sc.

Rnd 4: Ch 1, sc in FL of same sc as joining; ch 3, sk next sc; * sc in FL of next sc, ch 3, sk next sc; rep from * around; join. Cut MC. Finish off.

Rnd 5: Working in BLs of Rnd 3, join Color B in first sc of any corner 3-sc group, ch 3, 3 dc in same sc, ch 1, sk next sc, 4 dc in next sc, ch 1, sk next 4 sc, 4 dc in next sc, ch 1; * 4 dc in first sc of next corner 3-sc group, ch 1, sk next sc, 4 dc in next sc, ch 1, sk next 4 sc, 4 dc in next sc, ch 1, rep from * twice more; join.

Rnd 6: Sl st in next 3 dc and in next ch-1 sp, ch 3, beg corner in same sp; ch 1, (4 dc, ch 1) in each ch-1 sp to next corner; * corner in corner ch-1 sp; ch 1, (4 dc, ch 1) in each ch-1 sp to next corner; rep from * twice more; join.

Rnds 7 and 8: Rep Rnd 6. At end of Rnd 8, cut Color B. Finish off.

Rnds 9 through 50: Rep Rnds 3 through 8 seven times more, changing color on each repeat of Rnd 5.

Rnds 51 and 52: Rep Rnds 3 and 4.

Weave in ends.

INSTANT GRATIFICATION PURSE

Designed by Kathleen Power Johnson

Time to make: About 6 hours

SIZE:
10" x 9½".

MATERIALS:
11 oz. 100% rayon cord

Note: Photographed model made with Judi & Co. Cordé Pine

Crochet hook size I (5.5 mm) or size required for gauge

Bamboo purse handles, 7½" along straight edge

Four markers or safety pins

GAUGE:
3 dc = 1"

PATTERN STITCHES:
Front Post Double Crochet (FPdc): YO, insert hook from front to back to front around post of st indicated, draw up lp, (YO, draw through 2 lps on hook) twice: FPdc made.

Back Post Double Crochet (BPdc): YO, insert hook from back to front to back around post of st indicated, draw up lp, (YO, draw through 2 lps on hook) twice: BPdc made.

Hexagon Instructions:
(make 2)
Ch 4, join with a sl st to form a ring.

Rnd 1: Ch 3 (counts as a dc), dc in ring; (ch 1, 2 dc in ring) 5 times; ch 1, join in 3rd ch of beg ch 3: 6 groups of 2 dc and 6 ch-1 sps.

Rnd 2: Sl st in next dc and next ch, ch 3; * BPdc (see Pattern Stitches) in row below in each of next 2 dc, (dc, ch 1, dc) in next sp: V-stitch made; rep from * 4 times more; BPdc in row below around each of next 2 dc, dc, ch 1, join to 3rd ch of beg ch-3: 12 BPdc and 6 V-sts.

Rnd 3: Ch 3, * FPdc (see Pattern Stitches) in row below around each of next 2 BPdc, V-st in ch-1 sp of next V-st; rep from around; join.

Rnd 4: Ch 3, BPdc in row below around each dc and FPdc and work V-st in ch-1 sp of each V-st: 2 BPdc added on each side.

Rnd 5: Ch 3 , FPdc in each BPdc and work V-st in ch-1 sp of each V-st.

Rnds 6 through 10: Rep Row 4 once, then Rows 3 and 4 twice more.

FINISHING:
Place a marker at the halfway point on sides 1 and 5 of each motif.

JOINING MOTIFS:
Hold motifs with wrong sides tog, matching markers. Join cord by pulling a lp through inside lp of dc at marker on outer edge of Side 1, sl st into corresponding dc on other motif. ** Working along this edge, sl st into each opposite dc pair and into the inside lp of each corner ch; work last sl st in marker on Side 5.

Working along front piece of Side 5 only, sc into both lps of each dc, ending by working in first corner dc.

ATTACHING HANDLE:
Position handle along wrong side of Side 6 of first motif, ch 3, sc into corner ch and around horizontal bar of handle; continue working sc around handle in each dc across, ending with last corner ch of Side 6. Sc in each unjoined st of Side 1.

On back motif, work from ** in joining motif instruction above to first sc of first motif sl st in sc.

Finish off. Weave in ends.

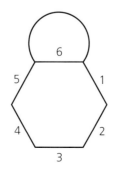

TRENDY TOP

Designed by Denise Black

Note: *Instructions are written for size Small; changes for larger sizes are in parentheses.*

Size:	Small	Medium	Large
Body Chest Measurements:	30"–32"	34"–36"	38"–40"
Finished Chest Measurement:	34"	38"	42"

Time to make: About 13 hours

MATERIALS:

Sport weight yarn, 9 (11, 13) oz, light green

Note: *Photographed model made with Patons® Grace #60230 Sweetpea*

Size F (3.75 mm) crochet hook, or size required for gauge

Size 16 tapestry needle

GAUGE:

5 sc = 1"

Instructions:

BACK:

Starting with bodice, Ch 86 (96, 108).

Row 1 (right side): Sc in 2nd ch from hook and each rem ch: 85 (95, 107) sc. Ch 1, turn.

Row 2: In first sc work sc, hdc, dc (shell made); *sk next 2 sc, shell in next sc; rep from * to last 3 (4, 4) sc; sk next 2 (3, 3) sc, sc in next sc: 28 (31, 35) shells. Ch 1, turn.

Row 3: Shell in first st; * sk next 2 sts, shell in next st; rep from * to last 3 sts; sk next 2 sts, sc in next st. Ch 1, turn.

Rep Row 3 until piece measures about 4" ending by working a wrong side row.

ARMHOLE SHAPING:

Row 1 (right side): Sk first st, sl st in next 2 (5, 8) sts; shell in next st; * sk next 2 sts, shell in next st; rep from * to last 6 sts, sk next 2 sts, sc in next st: 26 (27, 29) shells. Ch 1, turn, leaving rem sts unworked.

Row 2: Sk first st, sl st in next 2 sts, shell in next st; * sk next 2 sts, shell in next st; rep from * 22 (23, 25) times more; sk next 2 sts, sc in next st: 24 (25, 27) shells. Ch 1, turn, leaving rem sts unworked.

Row 3: Shell in first st; * sk next 2 sts, shell in next st; rep from * 22 (23, 25) times more; sk next 2 sts, sc in next st: 24 (25, 27) shells. Ch 1, turn, leaving rem sts unworked.

Row 4: Shell in first st; * sk next 2 sts, shell in next st; rep from * to last 3 sts; sk next 2 sts, sc in next st. Ch 1, turn.

Rep Row 4 until armhole measures about 6" ending by working a wrong side row.

RIGHT NECK AND SHOULDER SHAPING:

Row 1 (right side): Shell in first st; * sk next 2 sts, shell in next st; rep from * 5 (5, 5) times more; sk next 2 sts, sc in next st: 7 (7, 7) shells. Ch 1, turn, leaving rem 51 (54, 60) sts unworked.

Row 2: Sk first st, sl st in next 2 sts, shell in next st; * sk next 2 sts, shell in next st; rep from * to last 3 sts; sk next 2 sts, sc in next last st: 6 (6, 6) shells. Ch 1, turn.

Row 3: Shell in first st; * sk next 2 sts, shell in next st; rep from 4 (4, 4) times more; sk next 2 sts, sc in next st. Ch 1, turn, leaving rem sts unworked.

Row 4: Shell in first st; * sk next 2 sts, shell in next st; rep from * to last 3 sts; sk next 2 sts, sc in next st. Ch 1, turn.

Rep Row 4 until armhole measures about 8" (8½", 8½") ending by working a wrong side row. Finish off.

LEFT NECK AND SHOULDER SHAPING:

Hold piece with right side facing and last row worked at top, sk next 29 (32, 38) unused sts from right neck and shoulder shaping; join yarn with an sc in next st.

Row 1 (right side): In same st work (hdc, dc); * sk next 2 sts, shell in next st; rep from * to last 3 sts; sk next 2 sts, sc in next st-7 (7, 7) shells. Ch 1, turn.

Row 2: Shell in first st; * sk next 2 sts, shell in next st; rep from * 4 (4, 4) times more; sk next 2 sts, sc in next st: 6 (6, 6) shells. Ch 1, turn, leaving rem sts unworked.

Row 3: Shell in first st; * sk next 2 sts, shell in next st; rep from * to last 3 sts; sk next 2 sts, sc in last st. Ch 1, turn.

Rep Row 3 until armhole measures about 8" (8½", 8½") ending by working a wrong side row. Finish off.

99

continued on page 100

TRENDY TOP
continued

TRIM:

Hold piece with wrong side facing and beg ch at top; working in unused lps of beg ch, join with an sc in first lp.

Row 1 (wrong side): Sc in each rem lp: 85 (95, 107) sc. Ch 4 (counts as a dc and ch-1 sp) on following rows, turn.

Row 2 (right side): Sk next sc, dc in next sc, * ch 1, sk next sc, dc in next sc; rep from * across. Ch 4, turn.

Row 3: * Sk next ch, dc in next dc; rep from * across. Ch 4, turn.

Rep Row 3 until trim measures about 5½" (5½", 6") ending by working a wrong side row. Finish off. Weave in ends.

FRONT:

Work same as back until armhole measures about 3½", ending by working a wrong side row.

LEFT NECK AND SHOULDER SHAPING:

Row 1 (right side): Shell in first st; * sk next 2 sts, shell in next st; rep from * 6 (6, 6) times more; sk next 2 sts, sc in next st: 8 (8, 8) shells. Ch 1, turn, leaving rem sts unworked.

Row 2: Sk first st, sl st in next 2 sts, shell in next st; * sk next 2 sts, shell in next st; rep from * 5 (5, 5) times more; sk next 2 sts, sc in next st: 7 (7, 7) shells. Ch 1, turn.

Row 3: Shell in first st; * sk next 2 sts, shell in next st; rep from * 4 (4, 4) times more; sk next 2 sts, sc in next st: 6 (6, 6) shells. Ch 1, turn, leaving rem sts unworked.

Row 4: Shell in first st; * sk next 2 sts, shell

in next st; rep from * to last 3 sts; sk next 2 sts, sc in last st. Ch 1, turn.

Rep Row 4 until armhole measures about 8" (8½", 8½") ending by working a wrong side row. Finish off.

RIGHT NECK AND SHOULDER SHAPING:

Hold piece with right side facing and last row worked at top, sk next 23 (26, 32) unused sts from left neck and shoulder shaping; join with an sc in next st.

Row 1 (right side): In same st work (hdc, dc); * sk next 2 sts, shell in next st; rep from * to last 3 sts; sk next 2 sts, sc in next st: 8 (8, 8) shells. Ch 1, turn.

Row 2: Shell in first st; * sk next 2 sts, shell in next st; rep from * 5 (5, 5) times more; sk next 2 sts, sc in next st: 7 (7, 7) shells. Ch 1, turn, leaving rem sts unworked.

Row 3: Sk first st, sl st in next 2 sts, shell in next st; * sk next 2 sts, shell in next st; rep from * to last 3 sts; sk next 2 sts, sc in last st: 6 (6, 6) shells. Ch 1, turn.

Row 4: Shell in first st; * sk next 2 sts, shell in next st; rep from * 4 (4, 4) times more; sk next 2 sts, sc in next st: 6 (6, 6) shells. Ch 1, turn.

Row 5: Shell in first st; * sk next 2 sts, shell in next st; rep from * to last 3 sts, sk next 2 sts, sc in last st. Ch 1, turn.

Rep Row 5 until armhole measures about 8" (8½", 8½") ending by working a wrong side row. Finish off. Weave in ends.

TRIM:

Hold piece with wrong side facing and beg ch at top; working in unused lps of beg ch join yarn with an sc in first lp.

Row 1 (wrong side): Sc in each rem lp: 85 (95, 107) sc. Ch 4 (counts as a dc and ch-1 sp) on following rows, turn.

Row 2 (right side): * Sk next sc, dc in next sc; rep from * across. Ch 4, turn.

Row 3 (split row):

Left Side Trim: * Sk next ch, dc in next dc; rep from * 18 (21, 24) times more; Ch 4, turn.

Rep Row 4 until trim measures same about 5½" (5½", 6").

Left Side Trim: Hold piece with trim at top and wrong side facing; sk next dc from right front trim; join in next dc.

Row 3: Ch 4 (counts as a dc and ch-1 sp): Sk next ch, dc in next dc, * ch 1, sk next ch, dc in next dc; rep from * 17 (20, 23) times more, ch 1, sk next ch, dc in 3rd ch of turning ch-4. Ch 4, turn.

Row 4: Sk next ch, dc in next dc, * ch 1 sk next ch, dc in next dc; rep from * 17 (20, 23) times more, ch 1, sk next ch, dc in 3rd ch of beg ch-4. Ch 4, turn.

Rep Row 4 until piece measures same as right front trim. Finish off and weave in all ends.

ASSEMBLY:
Sew shoulder seams. Sew side seams.

TIE:
Make a ch that measures 50". Sl st in each ch. Weave tie through first row of trim.

EDGINGS:
Neck Edging:
Hold top with neck opening at top and right side facing; join with an sc in left shoulder seam.

Rnd 1 (right side): Working in ends of rows and each st, sc in each row to last 2 rows; dec over last 2 rows (to work dec: draw up lp in next sts indicated, YO and draw through all 3 lps on hook: dec made); dec over next 2 sts; sc in each st across to last 2 sts, dec in next 2 sts; dec over next 2 rows, working in ends of rows, in each st and next seam, sc to first sc; join in first sc.

Rnd 2: Ch 1, sc in same sc and in each rem sc; join in first sc. Finish off. Weave in ends.

Armhole Edging:
Hold top with right side facing and one sleeve opening at top; join with an sc in side seam.

Rnd 1 (right side): Working in ends of rows and in each st sc around sleeve opening; join in first sc.

Rnd 2: Ch 1, sc in same sc and each rem sc; join. Finish off. Weave in ends.

Bottom Trim Edging:
Hold top with right side facing and bottom edge at top; join with an sc in first ch-1 sp at left bottom opening.

Rnd 1 (right side): Sc in each ch-1 sp and each dc across bottom edge to ch-1 sp at right bottom opening, working along right front edge in ends of rows, work 2 sc in each row; working in any unworked sts, and ch-1 sps of first row of trim sc in each st and ch-1 sp; working in ends of rows along left front edge, 2 sc in each row; join in first sc.

Rnd 2: Ch 1, sc in same sc and in each rem sc; join in first sc. Finish off. Weave in ends.

BLACK TIE PURSE

Designed by Sandy Scoville

Time to make: About 6 hours

SIZE:

11" x 6½"

MATERIALS:

Worsted weight chenille yarn, 150 yds,
eyelash yarn, 20 yds black

Note: *Photographed model made with
Crystal Palace Yarns Cotton Chenille,
#2591 Grey, and Fizz, #7321 black*

Size G (4 mm) crochet hook, or size
required for gauge

Size 16 tapestry needle

One pair 6" wide plastic purse handles,
black

One pre-made 2" wide ribbon bow, black

Sewing needle and matching thread

GAUGE:

4 sc = 1"

Instructions:

FRONT

Starting at top edge with grey, ch 31.

Row 1 (right side)**:** Sc in 2nd ch from hook
and in each rem ch: 30 sc. Ch 1, turn.

Rows 2 through 4: Sc in each sc. At end
of Row 4, join black by drawing lp through;
cut grey. Ch 1, turn.

Rows 5 through 8: Sc in each sc. Ch 1,
turn. At end of Row 8, join grey by drawing
lp through; cut black. Ch 1, turn.

Rows 9 through 12: Sc in each sc. Ch 1,
turn.

Row 13: Sc in first sc, 2 sc in next sc; * sc
in next sc, 2 sc in next sc; rep from * across:
45 sc. Ch 2 (counts as first hdc on following
rows), turn.

Row 14: Hdc in first sc and in next 43 sc;
2 hdc in next sc: 47 hdc. Ch 2, turn.

Rows 15 through 22: Hdc in first hdc,
in each rem hdc, and in 2nd ch of turning
ch-2. Ch 1, turn.

BOTTOM:

Row 1 (right side)**:** Working in BLs only,
sc in each hdc. Ch 1, turn.

Rows 2 through 6: Sc in each sc. Ch 1,
turn.

Note: *At end of Row 6, do not ch 1.*

Finish off.

BACK:

Work same as front through Row 22.

Note: *At end of Row 22, do not ch 1.*

Finish off. Weave in ends.

FINISHING:

Step 1: Hold front and back with right
sides together; carefully matching sts on
last row of bottom and last row of back,
sew together through back loops.

Step 2: Fold bottom in half lengthwise;
with tapestry needle and grey, sew ½ of
one short end of bottom to side edge of
front and ½ to side edge of back; repeat
on other short end. Sew side seams with
matching yarns, leaving open at top edge
above black band.

Step 3: With tapestry needle and grey, sew
handles to inside top edges of front and
back just above black band.

Step 4: With sewing needle and matching
thread, tack bow to front above black
band.

HUGGABLE AFGHAN

Time to make: About 10 hours

SIZE:
44" x 54"

MATERIALS:
Bulky-weight chenille yarn,
  750 yards, blue
Note: *Photographed model made
  with Lion Brand Chenille Thick &
  Quick®, #109 Royal Blue*
Size P (10 mm) crochet hook,
  or size required for gauge

GAUGE:
10 sc = 6"
3 sc rows = 2"

Instructions:
Loosely ch 71.

Row 1: Sc in 2nd ch from hook
and in each rem ch: 70 sc. Ch 1,
turn.

Row 2: Sc in each sc. Ch 1, turn.

Rows 3 through 5: Rep Row 2.

Row 6: Sc in each sc. Ch 3 (counts as
first dc of next row throughout), turn.

Row 7: Dc in each sc. Ch 1, turn.

Row 8: Sc in each dc. Ch 3, turn.

Rep Row 7 and 8 until piece measures
about 50" from beg ch, ending by working
a Row 7. Work 6 rows in sc. Finish off.

103

CRAYON BLOCKS

Designed by Sandy Scoville

Note: *Instructions are written for size 2; changes for sizes 4 and 6 are in parentheses.*

Sizes:	2	4	6
Finished Garment Chest Measurement:	27"	28½"	30"

Time to make: About 14 hours

MATERIALS:

Sport weight yarn, 2¾ (3, 3½) oz Red; 2 (2, 2) oz each, green and white
Size G (4 mm) crochet hook, or size required for gauge
Size 18 tapestry needle

GAUGE:

5 dc = 1"
2 dc rows = 1"

Instructions:

BACK:

Note: *Back is worked with red only.*

Ribbing:

With red, ch 11.

Row 1 (right side)**:** Sc in 2nd ch from hook and in each rem ch–10 sc. Ch 1, turn.

Row 2: Working in BLs only, sc in each sc. Ch 1, turn.

Rows 3 through 50 (54, 56): Rep Row 2. At end of last row, ch 1, do not turn.

Foundation Row:

Working along side edge of ribbing, sc in end of each row: 50 (54, 56) sc. Ch 3 (counts as first dc on following rows), turn.

Body:

For Sizes Small and Large Only:

Row 1 (right side)**:** Dc in BL (back loop) of first sc, [dc in FL of next sc, dc in BL of next sc, dc in FL (front loop) of next sc, dc in BL of same sc] 16 (18) times; dc in FL of next sc, dc in BL of same sc: 68 (76) dc. Ch 3 (counts as first dc on following rows), turn.

Row 2: Dc in BL of next dc; * dc in FL of next dc, dc in BL of next dc; rep from * to turning ch; dc in 3rd ch of turning ch-3. Ch 3, turn.

Continue with All Sizes below.

For Size Medium Only:

Row 1 (right side)**:** Dc in BL of first dc, [dc in FL of next sc, dc in BL of next sc, dc in FL of same sc] 17 times; dc in BL of next sc, dc in FL of next sc: 72 dc. Ch 3 (counts as first dc on following rows), turn.

Row 2: * Dc in FL of next dc, dc in BL of next dc; rep from * to turning ch; dc in 3rd ch of turning ch-3. Ch 3, turn.

For All Sizes:

Rows 3 through 27 (27, 29): Rep Row 2 on 68 (72, 76) dc.

NECKLINE SHAPING:

Row 28 (28, 30): Work in patt over next 18 (20, 20) dc; dec over next 2 dc [to work dec: (YO, draw up lp in next dc, YO, draw through 2 lps on hook) twice, YO and draw through all 3 lps on hook: dec made]; ch 1, sc in side of dec just made; sc in next 26 (26, 30) dc, dec over next 2 dc; work in patt over next 18 (20, 20) dc; dc in 3rd ch of turning ch-3. Finish off.

FRONT:

Work ribbing same as for back.

Foundation Row:

Working along side edge of ribbing, sc in end of each row: 50 (54, 56) sc. Finish off red; join white with a sl st in last sc, ch 3 with white, turn.

BODY:

For Sizes Small and Large Only:

Row 1 (right side)**:** With white, dc in BL of first sc; (dc in FL of next sc, dc in BL of next sc, dc in FL of next sc, dc in BL of same sc) 8 (9) times; join red, drop white to wrong side of work; with red, (dc in FL of next sc, dc in BL of same sc, dc in FL of next sc, dc in BL of next sc) 8 (9) times; dc in FL of next sc, dc in BL of same sc: 68 (76) dc. Ch 3 (counts as first dc on following rows), turn.

For Size Medium Only:

Row 1 (right side): With white, dc in BL of first sc; (dc in FL of next sc, dc in BL of next sc, dc in FL of next sc, dc in BL of same sc) 8 times, dc in FL of next sc, dc in BL of next sc; join red, drop white to wrong side of work. With red, dc in FL of next sc, dc in BL of same sc, (dc in FL of next sc, dc in BL of same sc, dc in FL of next sc, dc in BL of next sc) 8 times; dc in FL of next sc, dc in BL of same sc: 72 dc. Ch 3 (counts as first dc on following rows), turn.

For All Sizes:

Row 2: With red, (dc in BL of next dc, dc in FL of next dc) 16 (17, 18) times; dc in BL of next dc; drop red to wrong side of work; with white, dc in FL of next dc, (dc in BL of next dc, dc in FL of next dc) 16 (17, 18) times; dc in 3rd ch of turning ch-3. Ch 3, turn.

Row 3: With white, dc in BL of next dc, (dc in FL of next dc, dc in BL of same dc) 16 (17, 18) times; drop white to wrong side of work; with red, (dc in FL of next dc, dc in BL of next dc) 16 (17, 18) times; dc in FL of next dc and in 3rd ch of turning ch-3. Ch 3, turn.

Rows 4 through 11 (11, 13): Rep Rows 2 and 3.

Row 12 (12, 14): Rep Row 2. At end of Row 12, cut white and red. Join green. Ch 3, turn.

Row 13 (13, 15): With green, dc in BL of next dc, (dc in FL of next dc, dc in BL of same dc) 16 (17, 18) times; drop green to wrong side of work; join white; with white, (dc in FL of next dc, dc in BL of next dc) 16 (17, 18) times; dc in FL of next dc and in 3rd ch of turning ch-3. Ch 3, turn.

Row 14 (14, 16): With white, dc in BL of next dc, (dc in FL of next dc, dc in BL of next dc) 16 (17, 18) times; drop white; with green, (dc in FL of next dc, dc in BL of next dc) 16 (17, 18) times; dc in FL of next dc and in 3rd ch of turning ch-3. Ch 3, turn.

Rows 15 through 24 (24, 26): Rep Rows 13 (13, 15) and 14 (14, 16) 5 times. At end of Row 24 (24, 26), cut white.

LEFT FRONT SHOULDER AND NECKLINE SHAPING:

Row 1 (right side): With green, work in patt across next 20 (22, 22) dc; dec over next 2 dc [to work dec: (YO, draw up lp in next dc, YO, draw through 2 lps on hook) twice; YO and draw through all 3 lps on hook: dec made]: 21 (23, 23) dc. Ch 3, turn, leaving rem sts unworked.

Row 2: Work in patt across. Ch 3, turn.

Row 3: Work in patt across next 18 (20, 20) dc; dec over next 2 dc: 20 (22, 22) dc. Finish off, leaving turning ch unworked. Finish off.

RIGHT FRONT SHOULDER AND NECKLINE SHAPING:

Row 1 (right side): Hold front with right side facing you; join white in 23rd (23rd, 27th) dc from left side; ch 2, work in patt across. Ch 3, turn.

Row 2: Work in patt to beg ch-2. Ch 3, turn, leaving turning ch-2 unworked.

Row 3: Dec over next 2 dc, work in pattern across.

Finish off. Weave in ends.

SLEEVE (Make one red and one green):
Ribbing:
Ch 11.

Row 1 (right side): Sc in 2nd ch from hook and in each rem ch:10 sc. Ch 1, turn.

Row 2: Working in BLs only, sc in each sc. Ch 1, turn.

Rows 3 through 28 (30, 32): Rep Row 2. At end of last row, ch 2, do not turn.

Foundation Row:
Working along side edge of ribbing, dc in end of each row: 28 (30, 32) dc. Ch 3 (counts as first dc on following rows), turn.

BODY OF SLEEVE:
For Size Small Only:
Row 1 (right side): Dc in BL of first dc; * dc in FL of next dc, dc in BL of next dc, dc in FL of next dc and in BL of same dc; rep from * 8 times more: 38 dc. Ch 3, turn, leaving beg ch-2 at beg of foundation row unworked.

Continue with Row 2 below.

For Size Medium Only:
Dc in BL of first dc; * dc in FL of next dc, dc in BL of next dc, dc in FL of next dc and in BL of same dc; rep from * 8 times more; dc in FL of next dc, dc in BL of next dc: 40 dc. Ch 3, turn, leaving beg ch-2 unworked. Continue with Row 2.

For Size Large Only:
Dc in BL of same dc; * dc in FL of next dc, dc in BL of next

dc, dc in FL of next dc and in BL of same dc; rep from * 9 times more; dc in FL of next dc and in BL of same dc: 44 dc. Ch 3, turn, leaving beg ch-2 unworked. Continue with Row 2.

For All Sizes:
Row 2: * Dc in BL of next dc; dc in FL of next dc; rep from * to turning ch; dc in 3rd ch of turning ch-3: 38 (40, 44) dc. Ch 3, turn.

Rows 3 and 4: Rep Row 2.

Row 5: Dc in FL of first dc; * dc in BL of next dc, dc in FL of next dc; rep from * to turning ch; 2 dc in 3rd ch of turning ch-3: 40 (42, 46) dc. Ch 3, turn.

Row 6: Dc in FL of next dc, dc in BL of next dc; rep from * to turning ch; dc in turning ch-3. Ch 3, turn.

Row 7: Dc in BL of first dc; dc in FL of next dc, dc in BL of next dc; rep from * to turning ch; 2 dc in 3rd ch of turning ch-3: 42 (44, 48) dc. Ch 3, turn.

Rows 8 - 9: Rep Row 2.

continued on page 106

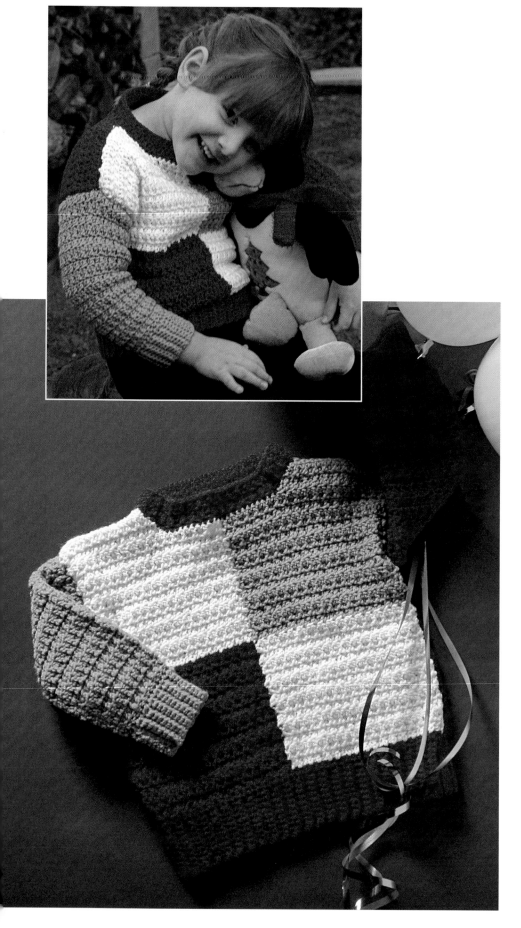

CRAYON BLOCKS
continued

Row 10: Rep Row 5. At end of row: 44 (46, 50) dc. Ch 3, turn.

Rows 11 - 16: Rep Row 6.

Sizes Small and Medium Only:
Row 17: Rep Row 7. At end of row: 46 (48) dc.

Size Small Only.
Finish off. Weave in ends.

Size Medium Only:
Row 18: Rep Row 2.

Finish off. Weave in ends.

Size Large Only:
Rows 17 - 19: Rep Row 6.

Finish off . Weave in ends.

All Sizes:
Sew shoulder seams.

Sew sleeves to body, matching center of last row of sleeves to shoulder seams.

Sew side seams.

NECK RIBBING:
Hold sweater with right side of back facing, join red in right shoulder seam.

Rnd 1: Ch 1, sc in same sp; working around neckline, sc in each dc across back, 2 sc in side of each dc row to front, sc in each dc across front, 2 sc in side of each dc row to beg, join in first sc.

Rnd 2: Ch 3 (counts as a dc on this and following rnd); dc in BL of next sc; * dc in FL of next sc, dc in BL of next sc; rep from * to last sc; dc in BL of next sc; join in 3rd ch of turning ch-3.

Rnd 3: Ch 3 (counts as first sc; dc in BL of next dc; * dc in FL of next dc, dc in BL of next dc; rep from * to last dc; dc in FL of next dc; join in 3rd ch of turning ch-3.

Finish off. Weave in ends.

THE LITTLE BLACK BAG

Designed by Sandy Scoville

Time to make: About 3 hours

SIZE:
About 8" x 8"

MATERIALS:
Worsted weight chenille yarn, 175 yds
  black

*Note: Photographed model made
  with Lion Brand Chenille Sensations®,
  #153 Black*

Size G (4 mm) crochet hook, or size
  required for gauge

Size 16 tapestry needle

One 3/4" diameter decorative black
  button with shank

One small pre-made black tassel

GAUGE:
4 hdc = 1"

5 hdc rows = 2"

Instructions
Starting at flap, ch 32.

Row 1 (wrong side): Sc in 2nd ch from
hook; * sk next 2 chs, 5 dc in next ch: shell
made; sk next 2 chs, sc in next ch; rep from
* 4 times more: 5 shells. Ch 3 (counts as
first dc on following rows), turn.

Row 2 (right side): 2 dc in first sc; sc in
third dc of next shell; * shell in next sc; sc
in 3rd dc of next shell; rep from * 3 times
more; 3 dc in next sc: 4 shells. Ch 1, turn.

Row 3: Sc in first dc, shell in next sc; * sc in
3rd dc of next shell, shell in next sc; rep
from * 3 times more; sk next 2 dc, sc in 3rd
ch of turning ch-3: 5 shells. Ch 3, turn.

Rows 4 through 39: Rep Rows 2 and 3.
At end of Row 39, do not ch 3. Finish off.

JOINING THE SIDES:
With wrong sides tog, fold first 8" up to
form front and back, leaving rem rows free
for front flap. Make lp on hook; join with
an sc though both thicknesses in side of
first row on one side edge; working along
side edge, work 2 sc in each dc and turning
ch, and one sc in each sc.

Work other Side Joining in same manner.

Finish off. Weave in ends.

STRAP:
Make 48" chain; fold and allow chain to
twist around itself.

FINISHING:
Step 1: Fold flap over to front. Sew button
to last row of flap. Attach tassel to button.

Step 2: Sew twisted strap ends to inside of
bag at side edges.

107

LITTLE FAN'S ONESIE

Designed by Denise Black

Size:	3-6 months
Finished Garment Chest Measurement:	22"

Time to make: About 8 hours

MATERIALS:

Sport weight yarn, 6 oz blue, 1 oz white

Note: Photographed model made with Patons® Look at Me, #6367 Bright Blue, and #6351 White

Size G (4.25 mm) crochet hook, or size required for gauge

Size 16 tapestry needle

Three 5/8" diameter buttons

Two white 2" sew-on numbers

Sewing needle and matching thread

GAUGE:

4 hdc = 1"

3 hdc rows = 1"

Instructions:

BACK:

Starting at back crotch, with blue, ch 19.

Row 1 (right side): Sc in 2nd ch from hook and each rem ch: 18 sc. Ch 1, turn.

Row 2 (buttonhole row): Sc in first 3 sc; * ch 2, sk next 2 sc: buttonhole made; sc in next 3 sc; rep from * across: 3 buttonholes. Ch 1, turn.

Row 3: Sc in each sc and ch across. Ch 2 (counts as an hdc on following rows), turn.

Row 4: Hdc in each sc. Ch 2, turn.

Row 5: Hdc in each hdc and in 2nd ch of turning ch-2. Ch 2, turn.

Row 6: Hdc in first hdc and in each hdc to turning ch-2, 2 hdc in 2nd ch of turning ch: 20 hdc. Ch 2, turn.

Rows 7 through 12: Rep Rows 5 and 6, 3 times more; at end of last row: 26 hdc.

Rows 13 and 14: Rep Row 6, at end of last row: 30 hdc.

Row 15: Rep Row 5.

Rows 16 through 20: Rep Row 6, at end of last row: 40 hdc.

Row 21: Rep Row 5.

Rows 22 and 23: Rep Row 6, at end of last row: 44 hdc.

Rows 24 through 40: Rep Row 5, at end of last row. Ch 1, turn.

ARMHOLE SHAPING:

Row 1 (right side): Sl st in first 3 hdc, ch 2 (counts as an hdc on this and following row), hdc in each hdc to last hdc and turning ch. Ch 1, turn, leaving rem hdc and turning ch unworked: 40 hdc.

Row 2: Sk first st, sl st in next, ch 2, hdc in each hdc to turning ch-2: 38 hdc. Ch 2, turn, leaving turning ch unworked.

Rows 3 through 12: Hdc in each hdc and in 2nd ch of turning ch-2. Ch 2, turn.

RIGHT NECK AND SHOULDER SHAPING:

Row 1 (right side): Hdc in next 8 hdc; dec over next 2 hdc; [to work hdc dec: (YO, draw up lp in next st) twice; YO and draw through all 5 lps on hook: hdc dec made]: 10 hdc. Ch 2, turn, leaving rem 27 sts unworked.

Row 2: Hdc in each hdc and 2nd ch of turning ch-2. Finish off.

LEFT NECK AND SHOULDER SHAPING:

Hold piece with right side facing and last row worked at top; sk next 16 hdc from right neck and shoulder shaping, join in next hdc.

Row 1 (right side): Ch 2, hdc in each hdc and in 2nd ch of turning ch-2: 11 hdc. Ch 2, turn.

Row 2: Hdc in next 9 hdc: 10 hdc, leaving rem hdc unworked. Finish off.

FRONT:

With blue, ch 19.

Row 1: Sc in 2nd ch from hook and each rem ch: 18 sc. Ch 1, turn.

Row 2: Sc in each sc. Ch 1, turn.

Row 3: Sc in each sc. Ch 2 (counts as an hdc on following rows), turn.

Row 4: Hdc in each sc. Ch 2, turn.

Row 5: Hdc in each hdc and in 2nd ch of turning ch-2. Ch 2, turn.

Row 6: Hdc in first hdc and in each hdc to turning ch-2, 2 hdc in 2nd ch of turning ch: 20 hdc. Ch 2, turn.

Rows 7 through 18: Rep Row 6, at end of last row: 44 hdc.

Rows 19 through 34: Hdc in each hdc and in 2nd ch of turning ch-2. Ch 2, turn. At end of Row 34, ch 1, turn.

ARMHOLE SHAPING:

Row 1 (right side): Sl st in first 3 hdc, ch 2 (counts as an hdc on this and following row), hdc in each hdc to last hdc and turning ch. Ch 1, turn, leaving rem hdc and turning ch unworked: 40 hdc.

Row 2: Sk first st, sl st in next st, ch 2, hdc in each hdc to turning ch-2: 38 hdc. Ch 2, turn, leaving turning ch unworked.

Rows 3 through 8: Hdc in each hdc. Ch 2, turn.

LEFT NECK AND SHOULDER SHAPING:

Row 1 (right side): Hdc in next 8 hdc; dec over next 2 hdc; 10 hdc. Ch 2, turn, leaving rem sts unworked.

Rows 2 through 6: Hdc in each hdc and in 2nd ch of turning ch. Ch 2, turn. At end of Row 7, do not ch 2, finish off.

RIGHT NECK AND SHOULDER SHAPING:

Hold piece with right side facing and last row worked at top; sk next 16 hdc from left neck and shoulder shaping, join in next hdc.

Row 1 (right side): Ch 2, hdc in each hdc and in 2nd ch of turning ch-2: 11 hdc. Ch 2, turn.

Row 2: Hdc in next 9 hdc: 10 hdc. Ch 2, turn, leaving rem hdc unworked.

Rows 3 through 6: Hdc in each hdc and in 2nd ch of turning ch-2. Ch 2, turn. At end of last row, do not ch, finish off.

SLEEVE (MAKE 2):

With blue, ch 31.

Row 1 (right side): Sc in 2nd ch from hook and in each rem ch: 30 sc. Ch 2 (counts as an hdc on following rows), turn.

Row 2: Hdc in each sc. Ch 2, turn.

Row 3: Hdc in each hdc and in 2nd ch of turning ch-2. Ch 2, turn.

Row 4: Hdc in first hdc and in each hdc to turning ch; 2 hdc in 2nd ch of turning ch: 32 hdc. Ch 2, turn.

Rows 5 and 6: Rep Row 3.

Row 7: Hdc in first hdc and in each hdc to turning ch; 2 hdc in 2nd ch of turning ch: 34 hdc. Ch 2, turn.

Rows 8 through 10: Rep Rows 5 through 7. At end of last row: 36 hdc. Ch 2, turn.

Row 11: Rep Row 3.

Row 12: Rep Row 4, at end of row: 38 hdc. Finish off.

ASSEMBLY:

Sew shoulder seams. Sew sleeves to front and back having center of sleeves at shoulder seams. Sew sleeve and side seams to leg opening. Finish off. Weave in ends.

EDGINGS:

Sleeve Edging:

Hold one sleeve at top with right side facing you; working in unused lps on beg ch, join white in seam.

Rnd 1 (right side): Ch 1, sc in joining, sc in each lp; join in first sc, changing to blue.

Rnd 2: Ch 1, sc in each sc; join in first sc, changing to white.

Rnd 3: Ch 1, sc in each sc. Finish off and weave in ends.

Repeat for other sleeve.

RIGHT LEG EDGING:

Hold onesie with right leg opening at top with right side facing, working in ends of rows; join blue in first row of back.

Row 1 (right side): Ch 1, work evenly spaced 25 sc along back leg edge; work 20 sc evenly along front leg edge. Finish off.

Row 2 (right side): Join white in first sc; sc in each sc. Ch 1, turn.

Row 3: Changing to blue, sc in each sc. Ch 1, turn.

Row 4: Changing to white, sc in each sc. Finish off and weave in ends.

LEFT LEG EDGING:

Hold onesie with left leg opening at top and working in ends of rows, starting with first row of front; join blue in first row.

Row 1 (right side): Ch 1, work 20 sc evenly spaced along front leg edge, work 25 sc evenly spaced along back leg edge. Finish off.

Row 2 (right side): Join white in first sc; sc in each sc. Ch 1, turn.

Row 3: Changing to blue, sc in each sc. Ch 1, turn.

Row 4: Changing to white, sc in each sc. Finish off and weave in ends.

NECK EDGING:

Hold piece with right side facing you and neck edge at top; join blue with an sc in left shoulder edge, working in ends of rows along left neck front, work 10 sc evenly spaced to front neck edge, sc in each st along neck, working in ends of rows along right neck edge work 10 sc evenly spaced, sc in seam, work 3 sc in ends of rows to back neck, sc in each st, work 3 sc in ends of rows to beg sc. Join in first sc. Finish off. Weave in ends.

EVERYTHING'S ROSIE JACKET

Designed by Denise Black

Note: *Instructions are written for size Small; changes for sizes Medium and Large are in parentheses.*

Size:	Small	Medium	Large
Body Chest Measurements:	30"–32"	34"–36"	38"–40"
Finished Chest Measurement:	36"	40"	44"

Time to make: About 14 hours

MATERIALS:

Worsted weight yarn, 13½ (15, 18) oz
Note: *Photographed model made with TLC® Amoré™, #3710 Rose*
Size I (5.5 mm) crochet hook, or size required for gauge
Size 16 tapestry needle
2 buttons, ½" diameter

GAUGE:

3 sc = 1"

Instructions:

BACK:

Ch 57 (62, 67).

Row 1 (wrong side): Sc in 2nd ch from hook and in next ch; * ch 3, sk next 2 chs, sc in next 3 chs; rep from * 9 (10, 11) times more; ch 3, sk next 2 chs, sc in next 2 chs- 34 (37, 40) sc. Ch 1, turn.

Row 2 (right side): Sc in first sc, sk next sc, * 5 dc in next ch-3 sp: shell made; sk next sc, sc in next sc, sk next sc; rep from * across to last 2 sc; sk 1 sc, sc in last sc. Ch 3 (counts as an hdc and a ch-1 sp on following row), turn.

Row 3: Sk first 2 sts, sc in next 3 dc (center 3 dc of shell); * ch 3, sk next 3 sts, sc in next 3 dc; rep from * to last 2 sts; ch 1, sk next dc, hdc in next sc. Ch 3 (counts as a dc on following row), turn.

Row 4: 2 dc in first ch-1 sp, sk next sc, sc in next sc; sk next sc, * 5 dc in next ch-3 sp; sk next sc, sc in next sc, sk next sc; rep from * to last sp, 2 dc in last ch-1 sp, dc in 2nd ch of turning ch-3. Ch 1, turn.

Row 5: Sc in first 2 dc; * ch 3, sk next 3 sts, sc in next 3 dc; rep from * 9 (10, 11) times more; ch 3, sk next 3 sts, sc in next sc and in 3rd ch of turning ch-3. Ch 1, turn.

Rep Rows 2 through 5 until piece measures 21" ending by working a wrong side row. Finish off.

RIGHT FRONT:

Ch 32 (37, 42).

Row 1 (wrong side): Sc in 2nd ch from hook and in next ch; * ch 3, sk next 2 chs, sc in next 3 chs; rep from * 4 (5, 6) times more; ch 3, sk next 2 chs, sc in next 2 chs: 19 (22, 25) sc. Ch 1, turn.

Row 2 (right side): Sc in first sc; sk next sc, * 5 dc in next ch-3 sp, sk next sc, sc in next sc, sk next sc, rep from *across to last 2 sc, sk 1 sc, sc in last sc. Ch 3 (counts as an hdc and a ch-1 sp on following row), turn.

Row 3: Sk first 2 sts, sc in next 3 dc; * ch 3, sk next 3 sts, sc in next 3 dc; rep from * to last 2 sts; ch 1, sk next dc, hdc in next sc. Ch 3 (counts as a dc on following row), turn.

Row 4: 2 dc in first ch-1 sp, sk next sc, sc in next sc; sk next sc, * 5 dc in next ch-3 sp; sk next sc, sc in next sc, sk next sc; rep from * to last sp, 2 dc in last ch-1 sp, dc in 2nd ch of turning ch-3. Ch 1, turn.

Row 5: Sc in first 2 dc; * ch 3, sk next 3 sts, sc in next 3 dc; rep from * 4 (5, 6) times more; ch 3, sk next 3 sts, sc in next sc and in 3rd ch of turning ch-3. Ch 1, turn.

Rep Rows 2 through 5 until piece measures 21", ending by working a wrong side row. Finish off.

LEFT FRONT:
Work same as Right Front.

SLEEVE (MAKE 2):
Ch 52 (52, 52):

Row 1 (wrong side)**:** Sc in 2nd ch from hook and next ch; * ch 3, sk next 2 chs, sc in next 3 chs; rep from * 8 (8, 8) times more; ch 3, sk next 2 chs, sc in next 2 chs-28 (28, 28) sc. Ch 1, turn.

Row 2 (right side)**:** Sc in first sc, sk next sc, * 5 dc in next ch-3 sp, sk next sc, sc in next

sc, sk next sc; rep from * across to last 2 sc, sk next sc, sc in last sc. Ch 3 (counts as an hdc and a ch-1 sp on following row), turn.

Row 3: Sk first 2 sts, sc in next 3 dc; * ch 3, sk next 3 sts, sc in next 3 dc; rep from * to last 2 sts; ch 1, sk next dc, hdc in next sc. Ch 2 (counts as a dc on following row), turn.

Row 4: 2 dc in first ch-1 sp, sk next sc, sc in next sc, sk next sc; * 5 dc in next ch-3 sp; sk next sc, sc in next sc; sk next sc, rep from * to last sp, 2 dc in last ch-1 sp, dc in 2nd ch of turning ch-3. Ch 1, turn.

Row 5: Sc in first 2 dc; * ch 3, sk next 3 sts, sc in next 3 dc; rep from * 8 (8, 8) times more; ch 3, sk next 3 sts, sc in next sc and in 3rd ch of turning ch-3. Ch 1, turn.

Rep Rows 2 through 5 until sleeve measures

about 5" (5", 5") ending by working a wrong side row. Finish off and weave in all ends.

ASSEMBLY:
With right sides facing sew shoulder seams from armhole edge in towards neck 5 1/2" (6 1/2", 7 1/4").

Holding garment with shoulder seams at top, measure from shoulder seam down 8" (8 1/2", 8 1/2") on each side and place maker on armhole edge. Matching center of Row 1 of sleeve to shoulder seams, sew sleeve between markers. Sew side seams to sleeve edges, leaving sleeve seams open. Repeat for other sleeve.

Fold back top front edges to make neckline Sew a button at each point to hold in place. See photo. Finish off. Weave in ends.

continued on page 112

EVERYTHING'S ROSIE HALTER

Designed by Denise Black

Note: *Instructions are written for size Small; changes for Medium and large are in parentheses.*

Size:	Small	Medium	Large
Body Chest Measurements:	28"–30"	32"–34"	36"–38"
Finished Chest Measurement:	32"	34½"	38"

Time to make: About 10 hours

MATERIALS:

Worsted weight yarn, 7 (9, 12) oz, rose
Note: Photographed model made
   with TLC® Amoré™, #3710 Rose.
Size I (5.5 mm) crochet hook, or size
   required for gauge
Size 16 tapestry needle

GAUGE:

3 sc = 1"

Instructions:

BACK:

Ch 50 (54, 58).

Row 1 (right side)**:** Sc in 4th ch from hook
(beg ch-3 counts as a dc); * dc in next ch,
sc in next ch; rep from * across: 48 (52, 56)
sts. Ch 3 (counts as a dc on following
rows), turn.

Row 2: * Sc in next dc, dc in next sc; rep
from * to beg 3 skipped chs; sc in 3rd ch of
beg 3 skipped chs. Ch 3, turn.

Rows 3 through 32: * Sc in next dc, dc in
next sc; rep from * to turning ch; sc in 3rd
ch of turning ch-3. Ch 3, turn.

Row 33: Sc in next dc, (dc in next sc, sc in
next dc) 5 times; sl st in next st: 13 sts.
Finish off. Skip next 22 (26, 30) sts, join in
next st, (dc in next st, sc in next st) 6 times:
13 sts. Finish off.

FRONT:

Ch 50 (54, 58).

Row 1 (right side)**:** Sc in 4th ch from hook
(beg ch-3 counts as a dc); * dc in next ch,
sc in next ch; rep from * across: 48 (52, 56)
sts. Ch 3 (counts as a dc on following
rows), turn.

Row 2: * Sc in next dc, dc in next sc; rep
from * to beg 3 skipped chs; sc in 3rd ch of
beg 3 skipped chs. Ch 3, turn.

Rows 3 through 33: * Sc in next dc, dc in
next sc; rep from * to turning ch; sc in 3rd
ch of turning ch-3. Ch 3, turn.

Row 34: Sc dec over first 2 sts (to work sc
dec: draw up lp in each of next 2 sts, YO
and draw through all 3 lps on hook: sc dec
made); * dc in next st, sc in next st; rep
from * to last 2 sts; sc dec over last 2 sts:
46 (50, 54) sts. Ch 1, turn.

Row 35: Sc dec over first 2 sts, * sc in next
st, dc in next st; rep from * to last 2 sts:
44 (48, 52) sts. Ch 1, turn.

Rows 36 through 45: Rep Rows 34 and
35 five times.

Row 46: Rep Row 34: 22 (26, 30) sts.

LEFT NECK SHAPING:

Row 1: (Sc in next st, dc in next st) twice;
sc dec over last 2 sts. Ch 1, turn.

Row 2: Sc dec over first 2 sts; dc, sc dec
over next 2 sts. Ch 1, turn.

Row 3: Sc dec over first 2 sts, ch 65, sl st in
each ch: tie made; sc in next sc. Finish off.

RIGHT NECK SHAPING:

Row 1: Sk 10 (14, 18) sts, join in next st;
ch 1, sc dec over first 2 sts, (sc in next st,
dc in next st) twice. Ch 1, turn.

Row 2: Sc dec over first 2 sts, sc, sc dec
over next 2 sts. Ch 1, turn.

Row 3: Sc dec over first 2 sts; ch 65, sl st
in each ch: tie made; sc in last st.

Finish off.

ASSEMBLY:

Holding back and front right sides facing,
sew side seams. Finish off. Weave in ends.

RED HOT PURSE

Designed by Sandy Scoville

Time to make: About 3 hours

SIZE:
About 8" x 8"

MATERIALS:
Worsted weight chenille yarn, 175 yds red
Note: *Photographed model made with Lion Brand Chenille Sensations®, #113 Garnet*
Size G (4 mm) crochet hook, or size required for gauge
Size 16 tapestry needle
One 7/8"-diameter decorative button with shank

GAUGE:
4 hdc = 1"
5 hdc rows = 2"

Instructions:

FRONT:
Ch 32.

Row 1 (right side)**:** Sc in 2nd ch from hook and in each rem ch: 31 sc. Ch 2 (counts as first hdc on following row), turn.

Row 2: Sk first sc, hdc in each rem sc: 31 hdc. Ch 2, turn.

Row 3: Hdc in each hdc and in 2nd ch of turning ch-2. Ch 2, turn.

Rows 4 through 21: Rep Row 3. At end of Row 21, ch 1; do not turn.

TRIM:
Rev sc in each hdc and in 2nd ch of turning ch-2.

Finish off. Weave in ends.

BACK:
Work same as front through Row 20.

Row 21: Hdc in next 14 hdc; ch 11 for button loop; sk next hdc, hdc in next 14 hdc and in 2nd ch of beg ch-2. Ch 1, do not turn.

TRIM:
Ch 1, rev sc in each hdc, in each ch, and in 2nd ch of turning ch-2.

Finish off. Weave in ends.

SIDE INSERT:
Ch 11.

Row 1 (right side)**:** Hdc in 3rd ch from hook and in each rem ch: 10 hdc. Ch 2, turn.

Rows 2 through 64: Hdc in each hdc. Ch 2, turn. At end of Row 64, do not ch 2.

Finish off. Weave in ends.

ASSEMBLY:
With right sides of front and side insert together, match the rows and sew them together using the tapestry needle and yarn. Work over the hdc and in each unused loop of the beginning chain, easing to fit.

Sew back to opposite side of insert.

STRAP:
Leaving 12" yarn end, ch 110; sc in 2nd ch from hook and in each rem ch. Finish off, leaving 12" end for sewing.

FINISHING:
Step 1: Fold insert inward at top of one side edge; insert one end of strap into fold about 1"; sew fold through strap to create pleat. Repeat on opposite side.

Step 2: Fold button loop over top edge of front and mark for button placement. Sew button to front.

114

THINK MINK

Designed by Denise Black

Time to make: About 45 minutes

MATERIALS:

Bulky weight yarn, 2½ oz brown

Note: *Photographed model made with Lion Brand Chenille Thick and Quick®, #227 Desert Print*

Size J (6 mm) crochet hook, or size required for gauge

Size 16 tapestry needle

GAUGE:

3 sc = 1"

Instructions:

Ch 6.

Row 1 (right side)**:** Sc in 2nd ch from hook and in each rem ch: 5 sc. Ch 1, turn.

Note: *Remainder of headband is worked in BLs only.*

Rows 2 through 5: Sc in each sc. Ch 1, turn.

Row 6: 2 sc in first sc, sc in next 3 sc, 2 sc in last sc: 7 sc. Ch 1, turn.

Rows 7 through 9: Sc in each sc. Ch 1, turn.

Row 10: 2 sc in first sc, sc in next 5 sc, 2 sc in last sc: 9 sc. Ch 1, turn.

Row 11: Sc in each sc. Ch 1, turn.

Row 12: 2 sc in first sc, sc in next 7 sc, 2 sc in last sc: 11 sc. Ch 1, turn.

Rows 13 through 20: Sc in each sc. Ch 1, turn.

Row 21: Dec over first 2 sc (to work dec: draw up lp in each of next 2 sc, YO and draw through all 3 lps on hook-dec made), sc in next 7 sc, dec over next 2 sc: 9 sc. Ch 1, turn.

Row 22: Sc in each sc. Ch 1, turn.

Row 23: Dec over first 2 sc, sc in next 5 sc, dec over next 2 sc: 7 sc. Ch 1, turn.

Rows 24 through 26: Sc in each sc. Ch 1, turn.

Row 27: Dec over first 2 sc, sc in next 3 sc, dec over next 2 sc: 5 sc. Ch 1, turn.

Rows 28 through 31: Sc in each sc. Ch 1, turn. At end of last row do not ch 1. Finish off.

Sew Row 1 and Row 31 together. Weave in ends.

Refresher Course in Crocheting

HOW TO CROCHET

CHAIN (ch)

Crochet starts with a basic chain stitch. To begin, make a slip loop on the hook leaving a 4" tail of yarn.

Step 1: Take the hook in the right hand, holding it between the thumb and third finger, and rest the index finger near the tip of the hook.

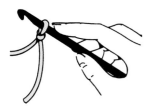

Step 2: Take the slip loop in the thumb and index finger of the left hand and bring the yarn over the third finger of the left hand, catching it loosely at the left palm with the remaining two fingers.

Step 3: Bring the yarn over the hook from back to front and draw through the loop on the hook.

You have now made one chain stitch. Repeat step 3 for each additional chain desired, moving your thumb and index finger up close to the hook after each stitch or two.

Note: *When counting the number of chains, do not count the loop on the hook or the starting slip knot.*

SINGLE CROCHET (sc)

First, make a chain to the desired length.

Step 1: Insert the hook under the top loop of the 2nd chain from the hook

Hook the yarn, bringing the yarn over the hook from the back to the front, and draw through.

Step 2: Hook the yarn and draw through 2 loops on the hook.

You have now made one single crochet stitch. To finish the row, work a single crochet (repeat Steps 1 and 2) in each chain.

To work additional rows, chain 1 and turn work counterclockwise. Inserting hook under 2 top loops of the stitch, work a single crochet in each stitch across.

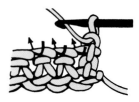

DOUBLE CROCHET (dc)

Begin by making a chain the desired length.

Step 1: Bring the yarn once over the hook; insert the hook in the top loop of the 4th chain from the hook.

118

Hook the yarn and draw through.

Step 2: Hook yarn and draw through first 2 loops on the hook.

Step 3: Hook yarn again and draw through last 2 loops on hook.

You have now made one double crochet. To finish the row, work a double crochet (repeat Steps 1, 2 and 3) in each chain.

To work additional rows, make 3 chains and turn work counter clockwise. Beginning in 2nd chain (3 chains count as first double crochet).

Work a double crochet in each stitch across, remembering to insert the hook under 2 top loops of the stitch. At the end of the row, work the last double crochet in the top chain of the chain-3.

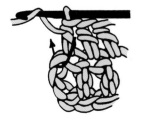

HALF DOUBLE CROCHET (hdc)

Begin by making a chain the desired length.

Step 1: Bring the yarn over the hook. Insert the hook in the top loop of the 3rd chain from the hook. Hook yarn and draw through (3 loops now on hook).

Step 2: Hook yarn and draw through all 3 loops on the hook.

You have now made one half double crochet. To finish the row, work a half double crochet (repeat steps 1 and 2) in each chain.

To work additional rows, make 2 chains and turn work counterclockwise. Beginning in 2nd stitch (2 chains count as first half double crochet), work a half double crochet in each stitch across. At the end of the row, work the last half double crochet in the top chain of the chain-2.

TRIPLE CROCHET (tr)

Begin by making a chain the desired length

Step 1: Bring yarn twice over the hook. Insert the hook in the 5th chain from the hook.

Hook yarn and draw through.

Step 2: Hook yarn and draw through the first 2 loops on the hook.

Step 3: Hook yarn and draw through the next two loops on the hook.

Step 4: Hook yarn and draw through the remaining 2 loops on the hook.

You have now made one triple crochet. To finish the row, work a triple crochet (repeat steps 1 through 4) in each remaining chain.

To work additional rows, make 4 chains and turn work counterclockwise. Beginning in 2nd stitch (4 chains count as first triple crochet), work a triple crochet as before in each chain across. At the end of the row, work the last triple crochet in the top chain of chain-4.

SLIP STITCH (sl st)

This stitch is used to join work or to move the yarn across a group of stitches without adding any height to the project.

Begin by making a chain the desired length.

Step 1: Insert hook in 2nd chain from hook. Hook yarn and draw through both stitch and loop on hook in one motion.

SINGLE AND DOUBLE LOVER'S KNOT

Step 1: Draw up a lp to length specified in pattern; YO and draw through lp just made.

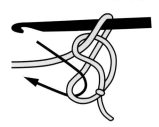

Step 2: Insert hook in back strand of long lp to left; YO and draw through, YO and draw through 2 lps on hook.

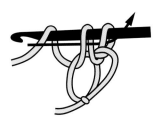

Step 3: Completed Single Lover's Knot

Double Lover's Knot
Rep Steps 1 and 2.

Completed Double Lover's Knot

EDGINGS

Single Crochet Edging: To make this edging, you will be asked to "keep your work flat". This means to adjust your stitches as you work. It may be necessary to skip a row or stitch here or there to keep the edging from rippling; or to add a stitch to keep the work from pulling in, When working around a corner, it is usually necessary to work 3 stitches in the center corner stitch to keep the corner flat and square.

Reverse Single Crochet Edging: This produces a lovely corded effect and is usually worked after a row of single crochet. It is worked on the right side from left to right (the opposite direction for working single crochet).

WEAVING IN ENDS

When you finish your project, all of the yarn ends should be woven in securely. To do this, use a size 16 tapestry needle or a plastic yarn needle and weave the yarn ends through the backs of the stitches, first weaving about 2" in one direction and then 1" in the reverse direction. Cut off excess yarn.

FRINGE

Basic Instructions
Cut a piece of cardboard about 6" wide and half as long as specified in the instructions for strands, plus ½" for trimming allowance. Wind the yarn loosely and evenly lengthwise around cardboard. When the card is filled, cut the yarn across one end. Do this several times; then begin fringing. You can wind additional strands as you need them.

Single Knot Fringe
Hold the specified number of strands for one knot of fringe together, then fold in half.

Hold the knitted project with the right side facing you. Using a crochet hook, draw the folded ends through the space or stitch from right to wrong side.

Pull the loose ends through the folded section.

Draw the knot up firmly.

Space the knots as indicated in the pattern instructions. Trim the ends of the fringe evenly.

Double Knot Fringe

Begin by working Single Knot Fringe. With right side facing you and working from left to right, take half the strands of one knot and half the strands in the knot next to it, and knot them together.

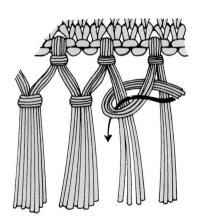

Triple Knot Fringe

First work Double Knot Fringe. Then working again on right side from left to right, tie the third row of knots.

GAUGE

This is probably the most important aspect of crocheting!

GAUGE simply means the number of stitches per inch, and the number of rows per inch that result from a specified yarn worked with hooks in a specified size. But since everyone crochets differently—some loosely, some tightly, some in-between—the measurements of individual work can vary greatly, even when the crocheters use the same pattern and the same size yarn and hook.

If you don't work to the gauge specified in the pattern, your crocheted projects will never be the correct size, and you may not have enough yarn to finish your project.

Hook sizes given in instructions are merely guides, and should never be used without a gauge swatch. Crochet a swatch that is about 4" square, using the suggested hook and number of stitches given in the pattern. Measure your swatch. If the number of stitches are fewer than those listed in the pattern's gauge, try making another swatch with a smaller hook. If the number of stitches are more than are called for in the pattern's gauge, try making another swatch with a larger hook. It is your responsibility to make sure you achieve the gauge specified in the pattern.

If a row gauge is given and you have the correct number of stitches per inch but cannot achieve the row gauge, adjust the height of your stitches. This means that after inserting the hook to begin a new stitch, draw up a little more yarn if your stitches are not tall enough—this makes the first loop slightly higher; or draw up less yarn if your stitches are too tall. Practice will help you achieve the correct height.

THREAD CROCHET

Most of the projects in this book are worked with yarn and a aluminum, plastic, or bamboo crochet hook. If you would like to make the doilies, however, you will need to know how to work with thread and a steel crochet hook.

Most steel crochet hooks are about 5″ long, which is shorter than the hooks you use for yarn. Steel hooks are numbered from 14, which is the smallest, to 00, which is the largest.

If you have never worked with a steel hook, the first few stitches may seem awkward, but you will learn to adjust to the hook. You will find that the steel hook is shaped differently from the hooks you have been using.

The end that is used to hook the thread is marked by the number **1**. Number **2** represents the throat, which will help you move the stitch onto the working area, which is indicated by the number **3**. The number **4** indicates the finger-hold and the handle is marked as number **5**. Every stitch needs to be made on the working area, not the throat. That would make the stitch too tight. If you work the stitch on the fingerhold, your stitches with be stretched.

The thread used for crochet comes in a number of sizes; the larger the number, the finer the thread. Size 10, called bedspread weight, is the thread most commonly used (and the one that is used here in the doilies).

Most thread projects require finishing. Wash the completed doily carefully by hand using a mild soap and rinse it very well in warm water. If your doily is not soiled, you may not wish to wash it; in that case, merely dampen the doily.

Spread the doily out on a flat surface. If you are planning to do many thread projects, you might want to invest in a blocking board. Making certain that the right side is up, smooth the doily out to its proper size. Make sure that all of the loops and swirls are open and in their right positions. You may want to pin the edges of the doily in place; in which case, use only rust-proof pins, or plastic or wood toothpicks. Some crocheters like to spray their doilies with starch to give the project some body. Be sure that the doily is completely dry before you remove it.

Some thread projects have a more finished look when they are starched. If you are planning to starch your doilies, you will need a stiffening solution. Commercial stiffening solutions are available at your local craft or needlework department or store. You can also make a stiffening solution from equal amounts of white craft glue and water.

Pour the stiffening solution into a plastic bag, and place the bag in a bowl. Wash and rinse your thread project, and immerse it into the solution. Allow the project to remain in the solution for about a minute. Then remove it, and press out the excess liquid. Don't squeeze. The project needs to be very wet, but no solution should be sitting in any of the holes.

Now place the project on your board and pin it in shape. Allow it to dry; removing the pins only when the project is completely dry. Be sure to use rust proof pins. If you cover your board with a sheet of plastic wrap, the completed project will be easier to remove.

Steel crochet hooks are numbered differently in the United States and the rest of the world. Here is a chart which will help to establish the difference:

STEEL HOOK SIZES

U.S.	00	0	1	2	3	4	5	6	7	8	9	10	11	12	13	14
METRIC	3.5	3.25	2.75	2.25	2.1	2	1.9	1.8	1.65	1.5	1.4	1.3	1.1	1.0	.85	.75

ABBREVIATIONS AND SYMBOLS

beg . . . . begin (ning)

Bl(s) . . . . back loop(s)

ch(s) . . . . chain(s)

CL(s) . . . . cluster(s)

cont . . . . continue

dc . . . . double crochet

dtr . . . . double triple crochet

Fl(s) . . . . front loop(s)

hdc . . . . half double crochet

inc . . . . increase

lp(s) . . . . loop(s)

patt . . . . pattern

prev . . . . previous

rem . . . . remaining

rep . . . . repeat(ing)

rnd(s) . . . . round(s)

sc . . . . single crochet

sk . . . . skip

sl . . . . slip

sl st . . . . slip stitch

sp(s) . . . . space(s)

st(s) . . . . stitch(es)

tog . . . . together

tr . . . . triple crochet

tr tr . . . . triple triple crochet

YO . . . . yarn over

* An asterisk (or double asterisks ******) in a pattern row, indicates a portion of instructions to be used more than once. For instance, "rep from * three times" means that after working the instructions once, you must work them again three times for a total of 4 times in all.

† A dagger (or double daggers **††**) indicates those instructions that will be repeated again later in the same row or round.

: The number after a colon tells you the number of stitches you will have when you have completed the row or round.

( ) Parentheses enclose instructions which are to be worked the number of times following the parentheses. For instance, "(ch 1, sc, ch 1) 3 times" means that you will chain one, work one sc, and then chain once again three times for a total of 6 chains and 3 sc.

Parentheses often set off or clarify a group of stitches to be worked into the same space or stitch. For instance, "(dc, ch 2, dc) in corner sp."

[ ] Brackets and **( )** parentheses are also used to give you additional information.

TERMS

Front Loop – This is the loop toward you at the top of the stitch

Back Loop – This is the loop away from you at the top of the stitch

Post – This is the vertical part of the stitch

Join – This means to join with a sl st unless another stitch is specified.

Finish Off – This means to end your piece by pulling the yarn through the last loop remaining on the hook. This will prevent the work from unraveling.

Continue in Pattern as Established – This means to follow the pattern stitch as it has been set up, working any increases or decreases in such a way that the pattern remains the same as it was established.

Work Even – This means that the work is continued in the pattern as established without increasing or decreasing.

Right Side – This means the side of the garment that will be seen.

Wrong Side – This means the side of the garment that is inside when the sweater is worn.

Right Front – This means the part of the garment that will be worn on the right-hand side.

Left Front – This means the part of the garment that will be worn on the left-hand side.

The patterns in this book have been written using the crochet terminology that is used in the United States. Terms which may have different equivalents in other parts of the world are listed below

United States	International
Single crochet (sc)	double crochet (dc)
Slip stitch (sl st)	single crochet (sc)
Single crochet (sc)	double crochet (dc)
Half double crochet (hdc)	half treble crochet (htr)
Double crochet (dc)	treble crochet (tr)
Triple crochet (tr)	double treble crochet (dtr)
Double triple crochet (dtr)	triple treble crochet (ttr)
Triple treble crochet (tr tr)	quadruple treble crochet (qtr)
Skip	miss
Gauge	tension
Yarn over (YO)	Yarn over hook (YOH)

CROCHET HOOKS CONVERSION CHART

U.S.	B-1	C-2	D-3	E-4	F-5	G-6	H-8	I-9	J-10	K-10½	N	P	Q
METRIC	2.25	2.75	3.25	3.5	3.75	4	5	5.5	6	6.5	9	10	15

Judith Brossart, Editor

Carol Wilson Mansfield, Art Director

James Jaeger, Photography

Graphic Solutions, inc-chgo, Book Design

All of the garments and projects in this book were tested to ensure the accuracy and clarity of the instructions. We are grateful to the following pattern testers:

Denise Black

Carrie Cristiano

Kathleen Power Johnson

Carol Wilson Mansfield

Sandy Scoville

We also extend thanks and appreciation to these contributing designers:

Denise Black

Kathleen Power Johnson

Carol Wilson Mansfield

Sandy Scoville

Whenever we have used a specialty yarn, we have given the brand name. If you are unable to find these yarns locally, write to the following manufacturers who will be able to tell you where to purchase their products, or consult their internet sites. We also wish to thank these companies for supplying yarn for this book:

Bernat Yarns
320 Livingston Avenue South
Listowel, Ontario
Canada N4W 3H3
www.bernat.com

Crystal Palace Yarns
2320 Bissell Avenue
Richmond, California 94804
www.straw.com

Judi and Company
18 Gallatin Drive
Dix Hills, New York 11746
www.judiandco.com

Lion Brand Yarn Company
34 West 15th Street
New York, New York 10011
www.LionBrand.com

Patons Yarns
320 Lvingstone Avenue South
Listowel, Ontario
Canada N4Q 3H3
www.patonsyarns.com

J&P Coats
Coats and Clark
Consumer Services
P.O. Box 12229
Greenville, South Carolina 29612-0229

Red Heart Yarns
Coats and Clark
Consumer Services
P.O.Box 12229
Greenville, South Carolina 29612-0229

TLC Yarns
Coats and Clark
Consumer Services
P.O.Box 12229
Greenville, South Carolina 29612-0229
www.coatsandclark.com

INDEX (bold face entries indicate pattern pages)

continued on page 128

INDEX

continued